# VOGUE & BUTTERICK'S
# HOME DECORATING
# PROJECTS

# VOGUE & BUTTERICK'S
# HOME DECORATING
# PROJECTS

Introduction by Nancy Fleming

A FIRESIDE BOOK
Published by SIMON & SCHUSTER INC.
New York London Toronto Sydney Tokyo Singapore

**F**

## FIRESIDE
### SIMON & SCHUSTER, INC.
#### Rockefeller Center
#### 1230 Avenue of the Americas
#### New York, New York 10020

*Editor and Senior Copy Writer* Jane Cornell
*Editorial Production Managers* Barbara Machtiger, Patricia Malcolm
*Project Consultant* Maureen Klein
*Senior Writer* Virginia Jansen
*Contributing Writers* Barbara Fimbel, Nancy Keller, Karen Kunkel
*Fabric Editor* Andrea Willis

*President and Chief Executive Officer* John E. Lehmann
*Publisher* Art Joinnides
*Senior Vice President, Editorial Director* Patricia Perry
*Vice President, Creative Director* Sidney Escowitz
*Fashion Director* Cindy Rose
*Technical Director* Janet DuBane
*Art Directors/Cover Design* Jeffrey Engel, Joe Vior
*Production Manager* Caroline Testaverde-Politi
*Technical Consultant* Joanne Pugh-Gannon
*Marketing Consultant* Mike Shatzkin

Book development, design and production provided by BMR, Corte Madera, CA
*Publishing Director* Jack Jennings
*Project Manager* Jo Lynn Taylor
*Electronic Page Layout* Donna Yuen

Printed in the U.S.A. by R.R. Donnelly
10 9 8 7 6 5 4 3 2 1
Library of Congress Cataloging in Publication Data
Vogue & Butterick's Home Decorating Projects/Introduction by Nancy Fleming.
p.    cm.
"Fireside book." Includes index.
ISBN: 0-671-88877-3
1. House furnishings.   2. Machine sewing.   3. Interior decoration.
I. Vogue & Butterick Patterns.   II. Title: Vogue & Butterick's Home Decorating Projects.
TT387.V64 1994                                                94-1208
746.9–dc20                                                    CIP

# To Our Readers

*Dear Reader,*

Home sewers have many bonds, but perhaps the strongest is our desire for creativity. As a school girl, I made my clothes out of necessity, since my allowance and taste in fashionable trends were not a good match. Soon I discovered the pride we all feel when responding to a compliment with the phrase, "Thank you, I made it myself!" Not only could I duplicate the looks I saw in fashion magazines, I could also individualize my wardrobe by choosing fabrics, colors, and accessories that worked best for me.

Sewing changed my life dramatically when I won the Miss America title using sewing for my talent presentation. The last line in my commentary was, "Have basic dress, will travel." This sign-off turned out to be extremely prophetic!

Through the years, my interest and skill in sewing have remained a way to express myself, whether sewing for my family, my television career wardrobe, my home, or crafts for gifts or charity bazaars.

The television series *Sewing Today* allows me an opportunity to combine many years of experience as a television show host and a home sewer. It is an exciting chance to meet the world's top designers in fashion, home decorating, and crafts. We hope to inspire you with the very best in contemporary design. Through the series and this book we also intend to increase sewing expertise with sewing information that utilizes professional techniques and the marvelous technology available today for home use. It's great fun for me to continue to learn more about something that has brought so much pleasure into my life, and it is an added joy to be able to share this creative process with you.

*Happy Sewing,*

Nancy Fleming

# Contents

# CHAPTER 1

# Getting Started

S ewing for your home is a natural extension for someone who sews apparel. It's as rewarding to dress your house as it is to dress yourself. Many sewing aids and equipment used in home decorating already are in the home sewer's workshop or closet. The tools are there, and so is the talent — yours!

You can brighten an existing interior or transform it entirely. Consequently, the projects in this book are designed to be undertaken individually or to be used together in a unified redecorating scheme all through the house.

# The Basics

## Set Your Style

The same style-savvy you use for dressmaking or craft sewing applies to home sewing, but in a different way. Scale and the distance from which you view most home sewing projects, especially window treatments, call for a new perspective. By mastering the information in this chapter, you will have the basics covered.

In many ways, you can create dramatic impact with relatively simple sewing techniques. Most home sewing projects do not have to be form-fitted, require few pieces, and are composed of straight edges and hems. And, you can create custom items through sewing, often saving a considerable sum.

Coordinating home sewing projects is much like accessorizing apparel. Consider the overall effect. Since you see the results of your home sewing virtually every day, you will want to have a comprehensive decorating plan that ties the elements together. See your home with new eyes. Walk from room to room making notes. Professional decorators make just such an audit, and use it in developing their schemes. Decide how well your rooms function now and how you could improve them. A bay window in the bedroom can become a wonderful reading area with the addition of a window bench nestled with pillows. An overlooked attic or basement area can become an entertainment center with a newly covered sofa and chairs.

Before deciding to get rid of the things that do not seem to be working, move them from room to room. Determine your own style. During your walk-through, list the furnishings you love, and those that now seem boring. These and treasured collections, artwork, and favorite colors are all clues to what style suits you best. Make sure that rooms blend with one another, or plan to adjust them so that they do. Most homes can accommodate a melding of your style with their own distinctive lines, and often the most successful means of creating a unified look is through the introduction of home-sewn projects.

Refine your plans. Shop in furniture and fabric stores and clip room ideas from magazines. Note your favorite colors and the combinations that have the greatest appeal. Start a swatch file for each room, attaching paint color, carpeting, and fabric samples. Include photos of each room, along with a list of needs and floor plan.

## Fabrics

Fabric combines the three elements that give a room life: color, texture, and design. The dominant *colors* in a scheme set its entire tone. *Texture* can intensify both colors and fabric design, adding a dimensional quality. Fabric *design* can lead the way to a contemporary plan or echo the comforting precedents of the past. Interaction of these three is so critical that you should consider them all in developing a scheme. When they work together well, they can bring drama, rhythm, comfort and a sense of life to your living area.

While you can strike out on your own, keep in mind that many fabric manufacturers have already coordinated fabrics into harmonious and exciting collections. Texture, colors, varying scale in prints are already designed to work with one another.

Remember that all elements used in home furnishing should be viewed from a distance. While you see the sofa's fabric up close, you also see it from across the room.

### FABRIC SHOPPING TIPS

- Carry a metal tape measure to check fabric design repeats.
- Make sure design repeats will work with your project.
- Check draping quality by gathering bolted fabric in your hands, and for a swag, hold at two points and drape.
- Stand back to see the effect both draped and flat.
- If possible, purchase all fabric you need from the same bolt, since colors may vary from one dye lot to another.
- Check fabric in indirect and direct light and under incandescent lighting to pick up texture or design diffusion and subtle color changes.
- Consider "railroading" fabrics, that is, cutting one long piece of lengthwise fabric rather than piecing crosswise. It may use more fabric, but save on seaming.
- Check that prints run true to grain. They should line up across the grain from selvage to selvage (cross grain) and run true along the selvage (lengthwise grain).

# Developing Color Schemes

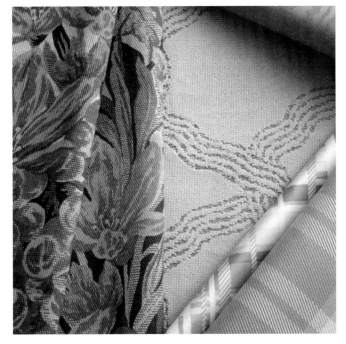

Elegant half-tones in plaids, solids, and floral fabric form a nicely blended color grouping.

Light colors are especially effective in darker rooms. Cool, light colors make rooms appear larger.

Bright colors are cheerful accents that bring life to a room. They energize, so use them judiciously.

Rich, dark tones warm up large spaces and can provide a regal and elegant ambience.

# Tools and Notions

Start with a large work surface, since most home decorating projects need ample room for cutting and pinning. Organize your tools and notions before you begin.

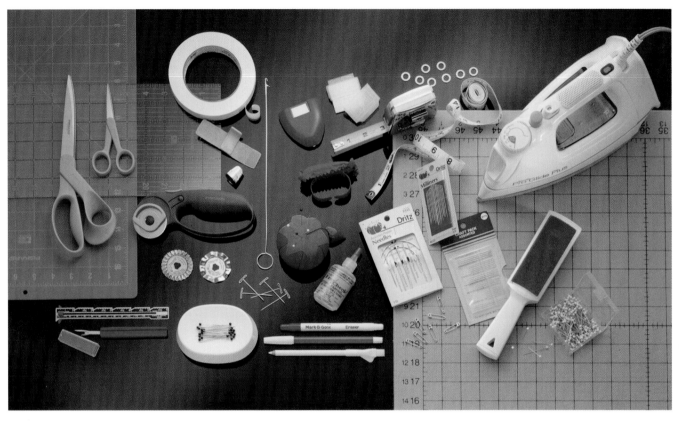

Many items used for dressmaking also are ideal for sewing for the home. Others, such as rotary cutters and boards, pressing boards and oversized rulers, are extremely helpful in preparing the larger fabric pieces often used in home decorating projects.

**Large work surface.** This is very useful for pressing and pinning. Make your own by covering a piece of ³/₄" (2 cm) thick 4' x 8' (122 cm x 244 cm) plywood for large projects. Another wonderful option is a Teflon-coated folding 33" x 52" (84 cm x 130 cm) gridded pressing and pinning board, or even more modest cardboard mat.

**Pressing.** Select an iron with a large steam surface and with excellent temperature control. Electric steamers are helpful for draperies and slipcovers.

**Measuring.** Metal tape measures are essential for hardware placements. Use a flexible tape measure to gauge angles and curves, and a 6" x 24" (15 cm x 61 cm) dressmaker's ruler or a T-square to establish square and bias of fabric, and quickly mark allowances on flat fabrics. A seam gauge is useful for measuring accurate hems and seam allowances.

**Cutting.** Use shears with long blades and bent handles that allow fabric to lie flat for more accurate cutting. Trimming scissors and a seam ripper are necessary for dealing with close work. A rotary cutter and self-healing mat are perfect for cutting straight panels and strips. Special cutting blades produce pinked or curved edges.

**Marking.** Chalk markers and new disappearing markers, either air-erasable or water-soluble, take the guesswork out of long lines.

**Pinning.** Safety pins assist in gathering ruffling, T-pins in securing heavy fabric in place. Glass- or plastic-headed pins are easy to locate on fabric. Use magnetic pin caddies and cushions to keep pins handy.

**Stitching and sewing.** Machine needles are available in various sizes to suit the weight of fabric being used. Specialty needles, such as wing needles, are required for some projects. Use a new needle for each project to ensure sharpness. Milliner's needles are best for hand-tacking and finishing. Thimbles and finger guards are helpful for sensitive fingers.

**Adhering.** Seam sealant will help prevent fabric from fraying. Fabric glue acts as a stabilizer to hold fabrics together. Use masking tape to hold fabric in position without leaving a residue, and fusible web or tape to heat-set two fabrics together for later finish stitching.

## Sewing Machines

Many home decorating projects are easily completed with straight machine stitching. However, when your machine has multiple capabilities, such as specialty stitches and ruffling, it is much easier to customize projects.

Sergers, also known as overlock machines, have the ability to stitch, finish, and trim in one step, making short work of many of the time-consuming aspects of stitching. They duplicate the professional seam finishes found in manufactured goods. A serger will not replace a sewing machine, but it will be an adjunct to it that many sewers will find useful.

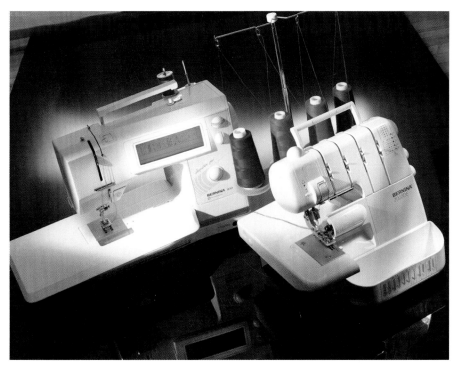

Two invaluable tools for sewing for home decorating are the sewing machine and serger.

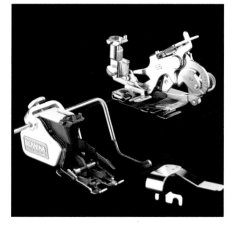

Specialty sewing machine feet appropriate for home decorating include, clockwise, from lower left: a walking foot (sometimes called an even feed foot), which feeds layers of fabric through at the same rate; a ruffling attachment for a sewing machine that gathers or pleats fabric and sews it to a flat piece in one step; a gathering attachment for a serger that performs the same task.

## Cutting Techniques

Having a large surface for cutting makes this step both easier and more accurate. Press fabrics flat before attempting any cutting. Make sure your cutting tools are sharp and that you have plenty of pins for holding fabrics in place. As you press, pin to mark the fabric lengths you plan to cut, to make sure you have enough fabric to finish the project. Re-measure and adjust these markings before cutting if necessary. Mark the top edge with an arrow pointing up to indicate fabric direction as you cut for future reference.

Cut all panels with print motifs lining up in the same place. This will automatically position motifs for a perfect match when seaming. Start by cutting one panel first, then layer it on top of the uncut yardage, matching up motifs at the cut, crosswise edges. Mark and cut new panel; repeat with all future panels.

Allover prints and solids such as broadcloth or chintz need to be squared up before cutting. To square, fold fabric in half lengthwise and align selvage edges. If the grain is straight across the fabric width, the fabric will lie flat. If the fabric is off grain, ripples or bubbles will appear. Adjust fabric before cutting. Check the square of print motifs after each length cut.

Selvages are tightly woven and may cause distortion. For projects with long seams, trim selvage edges before cutting fabric. Some fabric selvage edges tend to pull less and lay flatter than others. To test fabric, press along selvage to lower edge. If it appears to go slightly off grain but not enough to warrant removing the selvage, clip into it every 3" to 4" (7.5 cm to 10 cm).

## SQUARING FABRIC

Fabric that does not lie flat is not truly squared. Ripples indicate the direction in which the fabric is pulled.

To square up the fabric, pull it in the opposite direction of the ripples. Smooth and press fabric flat.

## MATCHING PRINT MOTIFS

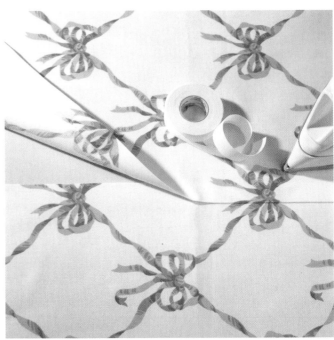

With right side of fabrics facing up, line up print repeat along selvage edges. Press one selvage to the wrong side. Apply paper-backed fusible tape just inside the pressed edge. Remove paper backing from tape, match motifs, fuse into position, then stitch in fold.

Use the same technique for matching motifs on fabric edges without selvages. Match design at seam allowances before cutting. Unfold fabric, stitch or serge fabrics together directly into the pressed line, trim, and press seam to one side.

# Seams

Take seam positions into account when planning your cutting. Avoid having a seam fall in the middle of a project unless it will be hidden by a pleat or fold. Projects such as tablecloths or duvet covers often require more than one fabric width. Create a wider panel by seaming selvage to selvage, right sides together, on either side of the center panel.

When stitching long lengths of fabric together for drapery, start at the lower edge and steam-press side edges together before pinning. This will help fabric hold together for stitching. Stitch from bottom to top along all seams, allowing any fractional differences to be adjusted at the heading. They will be least noticeable disguised by gathering.

A variety of seam finishes work well for home decorating projects. Master them on scraps before applying to projects.

**Zigzag finishes.** Trim seam allowance, press to one side and zigzag raw edges together.

**French seams.** Recommended for lightweight sheer fabrics and unlined window treatments, these seams also are known as clean finished seams.

**Serged seams.** Stitched and finished as one, these neat seams sewn on a serger take less time.

After seaming, finish raw edges to prevent fraying. Zigzag stitches and serging both can be used to finish individual edges. Press after stitching each seam, both front and back, to assure a smooth finish.

*Note: For clarity, stitching is often shown in a contrasting color in the photos throughout this book.*

Zigzag finishes, French seams, and serged seams all are often used in home furnishings projects. Another way to prevent edges from fraying is to turn edges to wrong side and straight-stitch or zigzag in place. If selvage is left on fabric, clip at 3" to 4" (7.5 cm to 10 cm) intervals.

To sew a classic French seam, with wrong sides together, stitch 1/4" (6 mm) from raw edges. Trim to 1/8" (3 mm). Press and turn fabric so right sides are together. Stitch 1/4" (6 mm) from fold, encasing first seam, and press to one side.

# Hems and Headings

At the lower edge of curtain and drapery panels, use a double 3" (7.5 cm) or double 4" (10 cm) hem. On the side edges, a 1¹/₂" (3.8 cm) double hem is the professional choice.

To turn a double hem quickly and easily, press the entire hem allowance to the wrong side. Open out and fold the raw edge to the pressed line and press. Hem as desired.

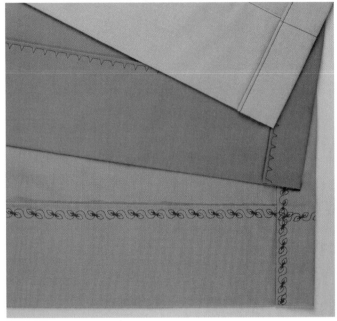

Top to bottom: Double hems are a quality custom window treatment finish. Stitch double hems with a straight stitch, blind-hem or a decorative stitch to accent the edge.

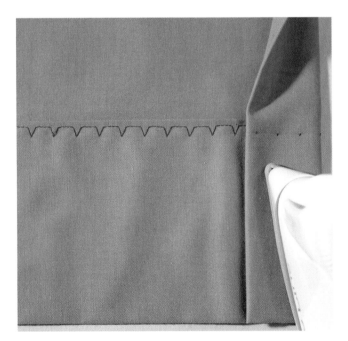

Turn side hems as for bottom hems, to make a 1¹/₂" (3.8 cm) double hem. To finish lower edge, leave a 12" (30.5 cm) length of thread and knot at the end of the stitching. Thread length onto a sewing needle and bury thread inside hem. Close lower edge opening with a slip-stitch.

For a single rod pocket, double fabric and allow ¹/₂" (1.3 cm) each for hem and rod pocket ease. Use a double hem for curtain header (extra fabric that forms a ruffle at the top when a curtain is hung) and rod pocket. Make a double hem the depth of the desired hem plus the rod pocket and ¹/₂" (1.3 cm) each for hem and ease along the rod pocket. Stitch above rod pocket to secure header.

## CUTTING CONTINUOUS BIAS STRIPS

To cut a continuous bias strip, cut a square of fabric and fold in half diagonally with edges even. Press diagonal fold and cut along pressed line. Pin straight edges (not the diagonal edges) right sides together and stitch with a $1/4$" (6 mm) seam allowance to form an angled rectangle.

Mark parallel lines on the right side from raw edge to raw edge. With right sides together, line up shorter straight edges. Match markings with one width of the bias strip extending beyond the edge, forming a tube. Stitch together with a $1/4$" (6 mm) seam allowance, turn right side out and press open. Beginning at one side, cut along markings in a spiral to form a continuous bias strip.

To cut with scissors, place tube around the end of the ironing board when cutting to avoid cutting underside. A quicker method is to use the cutting blade on a serger. Unthread the serger and line up the marked lines with the blade. The unthreaded needle will fall into the seam allowance of the bias strip.

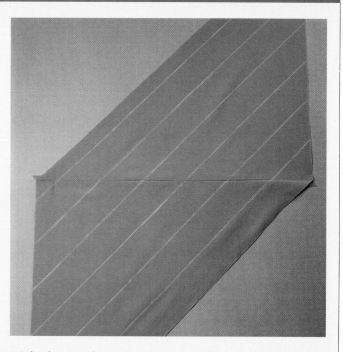

Stitch edges together and mark the width of strips needed from raw edge to raw edge.

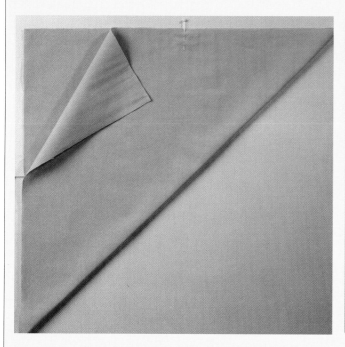

Cut a square of fabric and fold in half diagonally, press and cut along the fold line.

Stitch a tube and cut along the marked lines to make a continuous bias strip.

# Ruffling Techniques

Ruffles add a soft touch. Add a ruffled accent to a curtain or table topper, skirted slipcover, bedspread, or pillow. Although ruffles are decorative, their added weight will improve the hang of curtains and make pillows seem more luxurious.

Top to bottom: Ruffles are created with a zigzag stitch, a double row of machine-basting stitches, a serger, or a ruffling attachment. For outside applications, headers are finished to match ruffle hem, which can be finished in a variety of ways.

## MAKING RUFFLES

Ruffles can be cut on the straight grain, crosswise or on the bias. For long ruffles, use the lengthwise grain for less seams. However, ruffles cut on the bias will gather more softly and may be the best choice for some applications.

Cut strips two to three times the desired finished length or up to four times for wide ruffles and sheer fabrics. Cut the strip the desired width plus 1 1/4" (3.2 cm) for hem and seam allowances. Piece strip ends together diagonally if necessary. For a single ruffle, use a French seam to join strips with a neat finish. Narrow-hem or serge a rolled hem on one long edge and gather the other. If ruffle is being stitched on as a trim or sewn on top of an item, hem the ends and remaining long edge as a header before gathering.

For a double ruffle, cut the strip twice the width plus 1" (2.5 cm) seam allowance. If necesssary, piece strip ends diagonally. With right sides together, fold strip in half lengthwise. Stitch ends together if necessary. Turn right side out. Gather the raw edges.

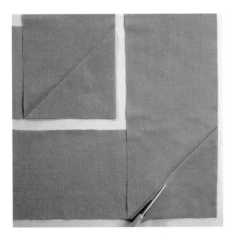

For diagonal seaming, with right sides together, overlap strips with raw edges even as shown. Strips will be perpendicular to one another. Fold corner of top strip at a 45 degree angle and press. Open out, and stitch along pressed line. Trim seam allowances to 1/4" (6 mm) and press open. For information on Cutting Continuous Bias Strips, see page 17.

## TIPS

- Add ribbon or other trimming to ruffles before attaching to project.
- Layer two ruffles for added fullness. Make the underneath ruffle the same size as the front ruffle, or deeper so that it shows. Finish hems on both ruffles identically, then stitch and gather as one.

## GATHERING RUFFLES

To gather ruffles, use a double row of machine-basting stitches, zigzag over cord, or use a serger stitch. Another option is a ruffling attachment for your sewing machine or serger that gathers and attaches ruffles in one step.

To machine gather, use a looser needle tension so bobbin thread floats slightly on the wrong side. Stitch a double row of basting stitches on the right side. Stitch $1/4$" (6 mm) and $3/8$" (1 cm) from the upper edge, or for a ruffle with a hemmed upper edge, stitch rows $1/8$" (3 mm) apart. Be sure to leave long thread ends and do not backstitch. Gently pull the bobbin threads while sliding the fabric along to distribute fullness.

For medium-weight fabric, use a gathering foot on your sewing machine and tighten the upper tension. This will gather the fabric as you stitch. Many sewing machines have a built-in gathering stitch.

A fast alternative method for gathering heavier fabrics and long strips is to stitch over a cord. With a zigzag stitch, stitch $3/8$" (1 cm) from upper edge over a thin strong cord, such as button and carpet thread, pearl cotton or dental floss. Set zigzag stitch wide enough to stitch over the cord without catching it in the stitches.

To gather on a serger, use a wide three-thread stitch and long stitch length. Serge upper edge of ruffle strip. Pull up needle thread to gather. Or, serge over a cord same as the zigzag method. If your machine has a differential feed setting, refer to your serger manual for how to gather with it.

After zigzag-stitching over cord, measure the finished gathered ruffle length and mark on cardboard or cutting board. Secure both ends of the ruffle to the markings with safety pins or T-pins and pull up thread to gather the ruffle to fit.

## ATTACHING RUFFLES

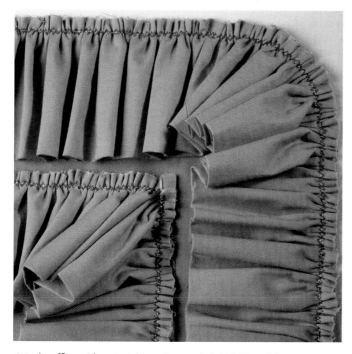

Attach ruffles with a straight or zigzag stitch $3/8$" (6 mm) from raw edge. Clip seam allowance to stitching to turn ruffle around corners. Ruffles can be stitched into a seam or applied to the surface.

For a quick hem finish, add a ruffle with a header. Press seam or hem allowances to right side. Trim to $1/2$" (1.3 cm).

To make a double bias ruffle with a header, cut and stitch strips together. Fold in half lengthwise with right sides together and raw edges even, and stitch along outer edges with $1/2$" (1.3 cm) seams, leaving an opening for turning. Trim across corners. Turn ruffle right side out and press. Slipstitch opening closed. Gather ruffle. Place gathering stitches of ruffle over seam allowance edge on right side of fabric and stitch in place along each side of gathering. Remove gathering stitches. If desired, add a flat trim or ribbon over gathering instead of removing stitches.

# Welting and Piping Techniques

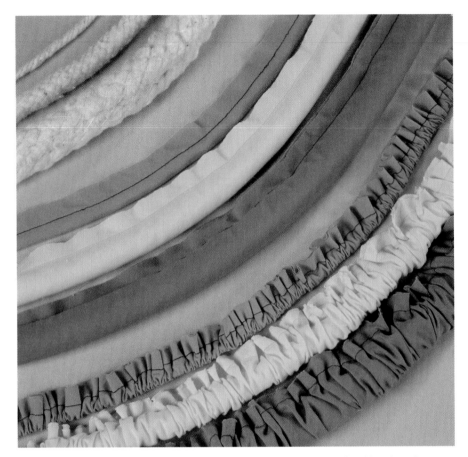

Welting or piping, sometimes called cording, can be made in a variety of widths, shirred or plain.

Welting refers to fabric-covered cable cord. With small cable cord stitched inside, it becomes piping; with larger cable cord, welting. Whether plain or shirred, welting or piping is a decorative and practical addition to slipcovers, duvet covers, valances, table toppers, and accessories. Welting strengthens seams, reduces wear on edges of furnishings and provides a decorative custom finish. Piping or welting can be purchased in various sizes or you can make your own by covering cable cord with bias-cut fabric strips.

To make welting or piping, use cord the length of the seam or hem plus 6" (15 cm) for ends. Cord is available from 1/8" (3 mm) in diameter to 1" (2.5 cm) in diameter. To determine strip dimensions, for width measure loosely around cord for the circumference and add 1" (2.5 cm) for seam allowances. Make strips the same length as the cord.

## MAKING WELTING AND PIPING

To cut a continuous bias strip, see Cutting Continous Bias Strips, page 17. With wrong sides together, finger-press bias strips in half lengthwise. Cut filler cord the length of the seam or hem edge. Place end of cord 3/8" (1 cm) from end of strip on wrong side of fabric. Encase cord with strip, matching raw edges. With a zipper foot, machine-baste close to cord without crowding it. Be careful not to stretch or pull the bias strip while stitching.

## ATTACHING WELTING AND PIPING

To apply welting, mark center of fabric where welting will be stitched. Place welting on right side of fabric with raw edges even. Place end 1/2" (1.3 cm) beyond center marking. Machine-baste in place, beginning 2" (5 cm) from center marking and being careful not to crowd the welting. To stitch welting into a seam, pin fabric right sides together with welting side up so basting stitches are visible. With a zipper foot, stitch 3/8" (1 cm) from raw edges, crowding welting or piping for a neat finish.

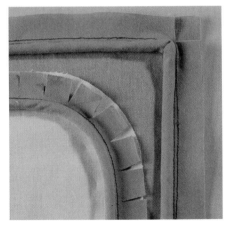

Around curves and at corners, ease and clip welting seam allowance to basting so welting lies flat. Clip corner at point where welting turns.

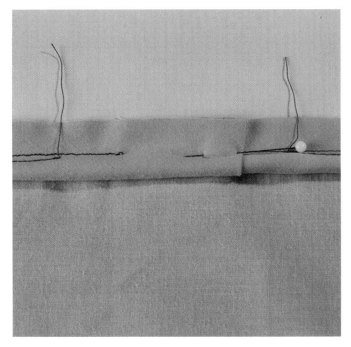

Stop stitching 2" (5 cm) from join. With presser foot down and needle in the fabric, cut welting so ends overlap 1" (2.5 cm). Remove 2¹/₂" (6.5 cm) of stitching from the welting and fold strip back. Cut cord so ends butt together. Fold one end of bias strip under 1" (2.5 cm). Overlap beginning of welting and cut strip. Continue stitching.

To stitch, pin both layers with right sides together and stitch from side with welting. Stitch with zipper foot as close to the welting as possible, crowding it. Trim all seam allowances to ¹/₄" (6 mm). For single layers, crowd as above.

## GATHERED OR SHIRRED WELTING

With a zipper foot, machine-baste welting, stitching across the end. Gently pull cord toward you, holding welting behind the presser foot and pushing fabric back until it is tightly shirred.

Shirred welting is a variation on basic welting and works best with a light- to medium-weight fabric. Cut strips with the grain rather than on the bias. Stitch cord and fabric together at one end to anchor cord. Fold strip over cord with raw edges even and with a zipper foot, machine-baste close to cord for about 10" (25 cm). With needle in the fabric, raise the zipper foot and gently pull cord towards you, holding the welting behind the presser foot and pushing the fabric back to the end until the fabric is tightly shirred. Realign raw edges and continue stitching and shirring fabric every 10" (25 cm). A leather roller foot also works well for this technique.

Apply shirred welting in the same manner as for other welting. Stop stitching 2" (5 cm) from center and remove from machine. Cut cording so ends butt together, stitch or glue to secure. Join welting ends. Stitch strip evenly close to welting.

# CHAPTER 2

# Window Treatments, Simple to Sumptuous

Windows are the frame to the outside world, and when lavished with special treatments, they can become a decorative focal point of a room or unify a space as secondary accents. Your choice of fabrics, colors, and textures determines the decorative tone of the room. Since many window treatments are based on straight panels, they are relatively easy to construct. This chapter shows you how to make simple unlined and lined curtains, a window scarf, a swag and jabots treatment, a shaped swag, a relaxed Roman shade, and more, all with custom workroom techniques.

# Window Basics

Consider the style of your windows first. Usually you will want to match treatments for windows within view of one another and to have them enhance the decorating style and architecture of your home. Be sure the treatment will not interfere with the window opening and closing. Also consider the possibility of energy-saving advantages from your window treatment.

## Window Illusions

You can visually reshape windows through your choice of treatment.
• Make a window appear higher and more impressive by adding a valance over the window.
• Make a window appear wider by extending the treatment on the sides beyond the window frame.
• Tame an overly-dominant window by placing a restrained treatment within the frame.
• Unify unmatched windows by having their respective treatments reach the same height and extend to the same level.
• Use a scarf to add a soft frame that leaves a view unimpeded.
• Block a dismal view with a gorgeous window treatment.

## Window Anatomy

Windows are best dressed when treatments end at either the sill or the end of the apron, or when they extend to the floor. Avoid hanging them to an unrelated length below the window. Widths extending one-third of the glass area to both sides of the window are graceful. Other widths also can be effective and can unify a group of windows.

Window details, such as the rails or mullions on window sashes, are all especially important for placement of tiebacks or half-window treatments. Finally, make sure the

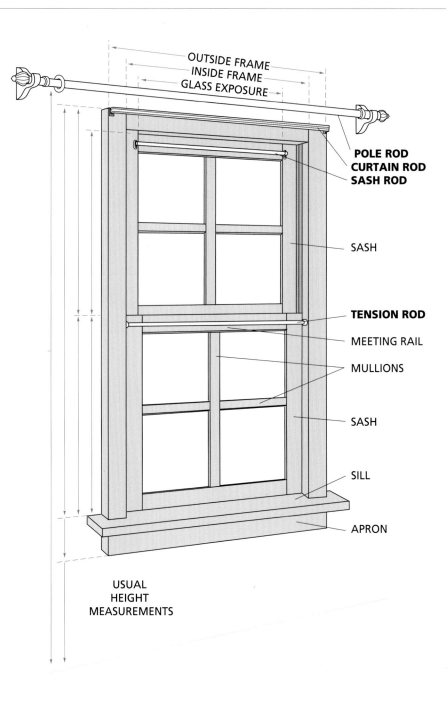

OUTSIDE FRAME
INSIDE FRAME
GLASS EXPOSURE

**POLE ROD**
**CURTAIN ROD**
**SASH ROD**

SASH

**TENSION ROD**

MEETING RAIL

MULLIONS

SASH

SILL

APRON

USUAL
HEIGHT
MEASUREMENTS

treatment is as effective from the outside as from the inside. For instance, you may want to raise shirring tapes, which are unattractive from the back, above the glass area of the window so that they do not show from the outside.

Sketch the windows you want to treat in scale to the wall on which they appear as an aid in developing a treatment. Add the dimensions that relate to your chosen window treatment, including window elements, floor, and ceiling. Use a straight or metal tape measure for accuracy. Treat windows in a room as a single decorative unit, measuring wall distances between them. Decide where to install the hardware for the treatment that best suits your needs and your window.

## Planning Custom Installations

Attention to detail in the beginning makes all the difference in the outcome of your window treatment.

• To preserve window frame molding, install brackets outside the window molding. Often, screws will go right into the framing studs for secure attachment.

• Mount top decorative rods so that decorative ring bottoms are at least 1/4" (6 mm) above window woodwork.

• Relate positioning of curtains to meeting rails or mullions on windows, if necessary. Install café rods at the same height.

• Check heating and air conditioning manufacturer's clearance recommendations for fabrics and flammable materials.

• If your windows are installed less than 12" (30.5 cm) apart, treat them as one unit.

# Determining Yardages

Choice of hardware and fabric will determine the amount of fabric needed to make curtains and linings. It will be easier to measure for yardage if you mount the hardware first. Estimate width first, then length, then make necessary adjustments.

## Determining Width

Measure curtain rod width from outside bracket to outside bracket, then add the projection of the bracket from the wall on each side to allow for the drapery return. This is the finished width the curtains are to cover.

For a conventional traverse rod, add an additional 7" (18 cm) for the overlap where the curtains meet. For a decorative traverse rod, measure from outside ring to outside ring, add the extension on each side to the center of the ring, then add 7" (18 cm) for the overlap.

**Stacking space.** For treatments wider than windows, allow for stacking space, the area where draperies go when they are drawn open, to partially clear the glass. Stationary window treatments mounted this way — often referred to as a stack back mounting — are great for making a small window look larger.

**Fullness.** After determining the width of the area to be covered, decide on the fullness you want,

---

### MEASURING WINDOWS

**Key Length Measurements**
• Ceiling to floor
• Ceiling to top of window frame
• Top of window frame to sill or end of apron
• Top of window frame to floor
• Meeting rails or mullion to sill or end of apron
• Sill to floor
• Inside frame, from top of window or mullion to sill

**Key Width Measurements**
• Outside frame to outside frame
• Inside frame
• Width of glass exposure
• Width of wall areas next to window that will be covered by the window treatment
• Width of wall areas between windows

based on the weight of the fabric. For lined or heavyweight fabrics, allow two to two and one-half times the width of the area to be covered. For sheer and lightweight fabrics, allow three times the width to be covered.

## FABRIC WIDTHS REQUIRED

To determine fabric width requirements, use this formula: Width + 6" (15 cm) x fullness ÷ by fabric width = number of fabric widths needed.

• Determine width to cover
• Add 6" (15 cm) for side hems
• Multiply by fullness (2, 2½ or 3 x width)
• Divide this by the width of the fabric
The result: The number of fabric widths needed to make the curtains.

Note: It is not necessary to include each seam allowance when figuring for curtains. However, include each seam allowance for flat treatments, such as Roman shades or box-pleated valances.

## Determining Length

The lengths you need to cut are determined by the overall finished length of the curtains, top treatment, allowance for a hem, and provision for matching prints.

**Top treatments.** Measure from top of rod to desired length, adding ½" (1.3 cm) for fabric lost if panels are gathered or shirred. Subtract ½" (1.3 cm) for casements or other fabrics that will relax and elongate when hung.

**Rod pockets (casings) and headings.** For rod pocket without heading, double the diameter of the rod and add ½" (1.3 cm) for easing fabric onto rod, plus ½" (1.3 cm) for turning under. For rod pocket with heading, double the diameter of the rod, add ½" (1.3 cm) for easing fabric onto rod, plus double the heading allowance, plus ½" (1.3 cm) for turning under.

**Curtain rods.** Measure from top of rod to desired length, adding ½" (1.3 cm) for the curtain to ride above the rod.

**Conventional traverse rods.** Measure from bottom of ring to desired length.

**Top and bottom installations.** Place rods equal distance from top and bottom of frame. Measure from top of rod to bottom, adding ½" (1.3 cm) for shirring loss for each rod.

**Hems.** Since valances and panels shorter than 48" (122 cm) look best with 3" (7.5 cm) double hems, add 6" (15 cm). Panels longer than 48" (122 cm) need 4" (10 cm) double hems, so add 8" (20.5 cm).

**Cutting length.** Adding all pertinent elements above to the finished length measurement of your draperies will give you the cutting length needed per panel, exclusive of print matching. Follow the advice of carpenters and always measure twice before cutting.

**Print matching.** Repeating print motifs or woven accents should line up along the drapery width. Often listed on the fabric selvage, repeats can vary in size. The larger the length of the repeat, the more fabric per panel needed for matching. To figure the cutting length, including print matching, divide the cutting length by the length of the motif. Round off and add to accommodate a complete

motif. For example, if the cutting length is 48" (122 cm) and the repeat motif is 10" (25.5 cm), round off the cutting length to six full motifs, or 60" (153 cm).

## Estimating Yardage

Multiply the cutting length by the number of widths required, then divide by 36 (100) to determine yardage (meters). Add extra fabric (at least a yard/meter) for testing and straightening.

## Linings

Consider the addition of a lining to your window treatment. It will add richer folds to curtains, and the additional weight will help them to hang smoothly. Linings protect fabric from fading and provide a harmonious view from the outside.

Panels shorter than 48" (122 cm) need 2" (5 cm) double hems. Panels longer than 48" (122 cm) need 3" (7.5 cm) double hems. For most applications, finish linings 1" (2.5 cm) shorter than the finished length of curtains and valances.

## TIPS

• Finish curtains and draperies that cover window moldings to 1" (2.5 cm) below the bottom of the window or ½" (1.3 cm) above the floor.
• Make valances to completely cover the window frame, except for an inside mount, and to a depth of 10" to 15" (25.5 cm to 38 cm) for most applications.
• Line up print motif repeats of matching wallcovering and window fabric.
• Match print motifs from the curtain bottom up. Position full motifs at the bottom hemline.

## HARDWARE CHOICES

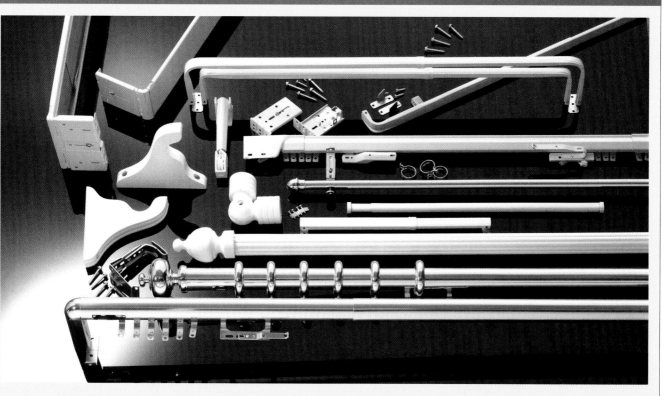

Hardware and where it is placed determines the overall shape and dimensions of a window treatment. It can be mounted on the ceiling, on walls, on the window frame, or inside the frame. Specialty hardware sets are available for almost any treatment. Here are some of the most popular styles. Mount all hardware following manufacturer's directions.

**Adjustable curtain rods** are usually hidden by fabric casings, called rod pockets, or covered with pinned headings. These rods are the basic window hardware, with variations that include transparent rods for use with sheers and flexible rods for rounded and arched windows.

**Wide pocket rods** are usually 2¹/₂" (6.5 cm) to 4¹/₂" (11.5 cm) wide, and make an impressive heading for a curtain or valance.

**Decorative pole sets** are available in many styles, and usually call for a flat application with no fabric return to the wall on each side. These rods can be used with rings for curtains or left plain to support swags, scarfs, valances, or shirred curtains.

**Sash rods** are designed to project a mere ¹/₄" (6 mm) from the mounted surface. These are often covered with gathered sheer fabrics, either in a single mounting or installed both top and bottom.

**Spring-tension rods** are used for mounting inside a window frame. They require no screws or brackets and are held in place by simple spring tension.

**Conventional traverse rods** are available in a two-way draw, in which the curtains are parted from the center, and a one-way draw, where curtains are pulled to one side. The rod itself is hidden and the pulley system works more smoothly than pull cords, especially for wide draperies. Rods also are available for bay windows.

**Decorative traverse rods** may come with decorative rings, while some utilize a hidden hanging system.

**Double-rod units** allow you to place draperies over sheer curtains, a valance over curtains, or to make any combination of layered and drawn window treatments. Double rods are designed for ideal clearances between layers. Installation is easier than using separate hardware and estimating clearances yourself.

**Tieback and holdback brackets** project from the wall and can be used to hold a scarf or swag in place or to hold curtains back from the window. Many styles, both plain and decorative, are available.

**Corner brackets** convert rods to a continuous right angle for corner window installations.

# Simple Unlined Curtains

Basic fabric widths, joined together and hemmed, are building blocks for the majority of window treatments. They are the easiest to make, which accounts for their popularity. Long, simple shirred curtains topped with a valance create a professional-appearing finished look, especially in a corner installation.

# Shirred Curtain

## CUTTING AND PIECING

Refer to Window Basics for determining window size, length of curtains, and number of widths required. For a valance no heading is needed. If the curtain will be used alone, consider a heading in addition to the rod casing. See Window Basics, page 26, for heading allowances. Stitch fabric widths together with $3/8$" (1 cm) seam allowances as necessary. Press seam allowances toward outside return edges to create minimum seam shadow lines.

## ASSEMBLY

Work from the bottom, then adjust at the top. Press lower edge hems up twice and hand-tack drapery weight at seam $1/4$" (6 mm) above bottom hem edge. Or, center a 3" (7.5 cm) beaded chain weight at each seam in the bottom hem fold and hand-tack in place. Press hem again, pin and stitch in place. At each side, press a $1^1/2$" (3.8 cm) double hem, then hand-tack drapery weight next to side hem edge, $1/4$" (6 mm) above bottom hem edge.

With weights in place, measure from bottom of curtain for precise curtain length. Estimate depth of heading, including rod pocket and seam allowance, and mark. Press

$1/2$" (1.3 cm) to wrong side along upper edge. Fold again to rod pocket line, press, pin and straightstitch

along folded edge. Install hardware and hang curtains following manufacturer's instructions.

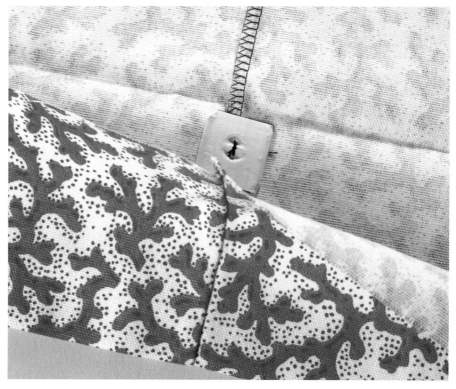

Hand-tack weights in place at each seam before finishing the hem.

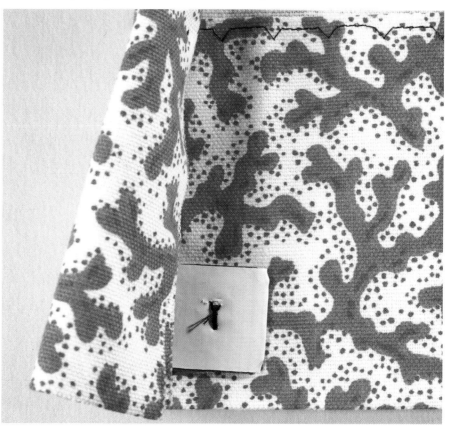

At corners, hand-tack weight on bottom hem inside side hems.

# Shirred Valance

The shirred valance is just a shorter version of the unlined curtain with a header. Adjust your measurements following the cutting instructions below.

## CUTTING AND PIECING

Decrease depth of bottom hem to 1½" (3.8 cm) doubled and eliminate the weights. Adjust for the most flattering placement of prints or lace motifs on the valance to coordinate with curtain beneath. Use matching fullness for curtain and valance.

When an even number of widths is required, split one width and add half to each side edge to prevent a seam from falling at the center of the window.

## ASSEMBLY

Estimate the height of the desired ruffle. To add a heading allowance, double the amount of heading, add rod pocket depth plus ½" (1.3 cm) and add the total to the length. Press ½" (1.3 cm) to wrong side along upper edges. With a ruler and chalk or disappearing marker, draw a line at top of heading and a stitching line between the heading and rod pocket. Fold upper edge down along heading line and pin. Stitch along rod pocket marking. Stitch lower rod pocket along folded edge. Install hardware and hang valances following manufacturer's instructions.

To keep stitching strong at hem edges and avoid cutting threads there, begin by inserting needle ½" (1.3 cm) from outside edge. Backstitch to just before edge, then continue stitching to opposite edge. Stop just short of edge and backstitch ½" (1.3 cm). Clip threads.

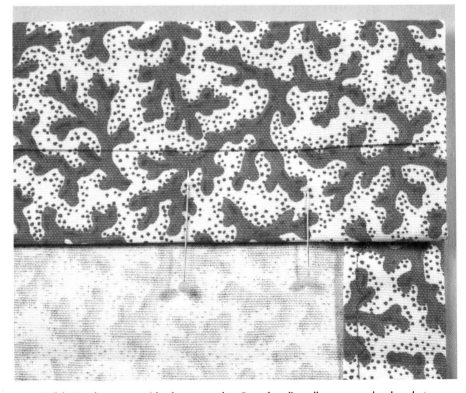

Press ½" (1.3 cm) to wrong side along top edge. Press heading allowance and rod pocket allowance to wrong side and pin in place. Stitch along upper rod pocket line.

# Arched Window Treatment

Fanciful as it may seem, this window treatment combines two simple curtain techniques—an arched curtain on top and a shirred curtain panel beneath, installed on both the top and bottom rods.

## CURVED WINDOW

The curved, or Palladian, window treatment begins as a straight panel. One long edge is shirred along the arched rod, while the other long edge is gathered into a rosette in the center of the semicircle.

Place curving curtain rod in window and adjust. Mark length from rod end to rod end, then lay rod out flat and measure distance. To determine length, estimate fullness of shirring (running lengthwise, or "railroaded," if you wish to eliminate seams in the fabric). Usually this will be 2 to $3^1/2$ times the rod length, depending on the weight of the fabric.

To determine fabric width, measure distance from top and sides of window to position of rosette at several points, and determine average distance. To this distance, add the following: $1^1/2$" (3.8 cm) for rod pocket; 1" (2.5 cm) for heading; $1/2$" (1.3 cm) for hem; and $3^1/2$" (9 cm) additional length to form rosette.

Serge or zigzag all edges. Fold $1/2$" (1.3 cm) then 2" (10 cm) to wrong side along one long edge for rod pocket and heading. Edgestitch

The header below and side seams lead directly to a wider than usual rod pocket that continues the double fabric framing of the window. A rosette finishes the upper curtain.

in place. Stitch $1/2$" (1.3 cm) from upper fold for heading. Place curtain on rod, adjusting shirring. Gather lower hem together at center of window, and secure with a rubber band. Adjust gathers and flair out rosette fabric. Secure rosette with buttonhole twist.

## SHIRRED PANEL

Match prints or lace motifs across fabric widths and seam panels as necessary. Make $1/2$" (1.3 cm) single hems on panel sides. Measure from top rod (bottom edge of Palladian curtain, which will overlap top edge) to lower rod position. At the upper edge, allow for a rod pocket plus $1/2$" (1.3 cm) for ease. At the lower edge, include 3" (7.5 cm) for a $1^1/2$" (3.8 cm) double header and rod pocket allowance plus $1/2$" (1.3 cm) for ease. Fold and stitch upper and lower rod pockets next to serged edge (no turn under needed).

Place panel on double rods following manufacturer's instructions. Hang and adjust arched curtain.

# Linings and Headings

Linings not only protect curtain fabrics and help them hang more smoothly, they also can be used as decorative accents to bring out the best in the curtain fabric. Be sure that when held up to the sunlight, the lining color does not distort the curtain fabric colors.

The simplest lined curtains are lined edge to edge and made by placing lining and curtain fabric right sides together and stitching around the perimeter, leaving an opening at the side edge for turning right side out, and then stitching for a rod pocket. An alternate is to use fusible tape to fuse the seam allowances together.

## MATERIALS

Figure yardage needed for your specific window (see Determining Yardages, page 25).

- Fabric
- Lining fabric
- Adjustable wide pocket rod

## MEASURING AND CUTTING

Determine the size of curtain. Make it at least 2½ times the width of the window to allow for ample turnback to expose the contrasting lining, including ½" (1.3 cm) seam allowances at each side. To length measurement, add 1" (2.5 cm) for ½" (1.3 cm) seams at top and bottom, and 3" (7.5 cm) for single header ruffle above rod pocket and an additional ½" (1.3 cm) for rod pocket ease.

Cut lining and curtain the same size, seaming as necessary. An alternate method, which allows lining to hang separately from curtain, is to allow additional lining length for a hem (see Linings, page 26). Turn and stitch hem on wrong side of lining, adjusting overall length so it is 1" (2.5 cm) shorter than the curtain. Add hem to curtain length, doubling the hem as if it were unlined.

Place lining and curtain fabric with right sides together, matching all edges. For alternate method, match edges at top and sides, but position bottom lining edge 1" (2.5 cm) above curtain hem as shown.

## ASSEMBLY

With right sides together, stitch lining to curtain with ½" (1.3 cm) seam allowances across top and along both sides, leaving an opening for the rod pocket. Turn right side out and slipstitch opening closed. For alternate method, turn curtain right side out through bottom hem opening. Trim corners and press curtain.

Leave rod pocket openings unstitched. When stitching around all four sides, leave an additional 9" (23 cm) opening below the rod pocket opening for turning.

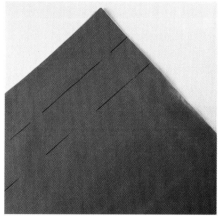

To make rod pocket, measure distance from top edge of curtain to top of rod pocket and mark with a disappearing marker. Repeat for lower rod pocket stitching line. Straight-stitch along marked lines, backstitching at ends.

# Banded Tiebacks

Vary the dimensions of tiebacks to suit the length and style of your curtains. Position them so they relate to the window elements, in this case, ending just above the mullion in the lower window sash.

turn right side out through opening. Press and slipstitch opening closed.

Sew a ring to tieback front ¹/₂" (1.3 cm) in diagonally from top corner edge. Attach a second ring to top corner of back.

Assemble bow strips in same manner as tieback without interfacing. Make a single knot at center of strip and tack in place at upper corner of tieback.

Stitch curtain and lining fabrics together along long edges. Press seams toward folded edge. Fuse interfacing to wrong side of lining.

## MATERIALS

- Small amounts of curtain and lining fabrics
- Fusible interfacing
- Plastic rings
- Tieback installation hooks

## MEASURING AND CUTTING

Attach hooks to wall ¹/₄" (6mm) in from outside edge of curtain and at desired height. Wrap a cloth tape measure around curtain and pin into place, adjusting to desired tieback length. Add 1" (2.5 cm) to length for seam allowances.

Cut two pieces of curtain fabric the length by 3" (7.5 cm) wide. Cut two pieces of lining fabric the length by 7" (18 cm) wide. Cut two pieces of interfacing the length less 1" (2.5 cm) by 4" (10 cm) wide.

For bows, cut pieces from curtain and lining fabrics 18" (46 cm) or longer by the same widths.

## ASSEMBLY

With right sides together, pin long edges of lining and curtain fabrics together. Stitch ¹/₂" (1.3 cm) seams along both long edges, leaving a 6" (15 cm) opening along one edge. Center curtain strip over lining strip and press seam allowances toward the outside edges, with 1" (2.5 cm) of lining fabric on either side of curtain fabric. Turn strip over and fuse interfacing to lining strip. Stitch ends with ¹/₂" (1.3 cm) seam allowance, trim corners, and

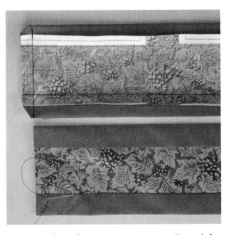

Stitch ends and trim across corners. Turn right side out and slipstitch opening closed.

# Hidden Linings

Linings add heft to lightweight curtains, prevent sun damage to fabrics, and have a clean look from the outside.

## MATERIALS

Figure yardage needed for your specific window, (see Determining Yardages, page 25).
■ Fabric
■ Lining
■ Drapery weights, if desired
■ Hardware

## MEASURING AND CUTTING

Cut and seam curtain fabric widths together as for Simple Unlined Curtains, page 29. Cut lining equal to the finished curtain width, matching any lining seams to curtain seams. To determine length, allow for a $1/2$" (1.3 cm) seam allowance at top and a 3" (15 cm) allowance for hem. Measuring from upper edge of rod pocket or pleating tape stitching line, make overall finished lining length 1" (2.5 cm) shorter than hem of curtain.

Butt seams of lining and curtain fabric and press seam allowances in opposite directions to eliminate bulk.

## ASSEMBLY

Press $1^{1}/2$" (3.8 cm) double bottom hems in both lining and curtain fabric and stitch in place. Press $1^{1}/2$" (3.8 cm) double side hems in curtains and open up. With wrong sides together, insert lining in curtain side hems from side edge to side edge. Hand-sew weights in place. Machine-blindstitch side hems, catching lining.

Press seam allowance, then rod pocket and header to wrong side over top of lining. Stitch in place, stitching through front and lining. Stitch rod pocket.

An alternate method for finishing the sides is to use a blind-stitch. After cutting and hemming, place curtain and lining fabric right sides together. Match seams and each side edge. Stitch $1^{1}/2$" (3.8 cm) seam allowances at each side. Turn right side out and press side hem seam allowances toward side hem edge, so that curtain fabric wraps to the back, overlapping $1^{1}/2$" (3.8 cm).

With right sides together, match lining and curtain raw edges at sides. Press $1^{1}/2$" (3.8 cm) to wrong side. Open out flat and stitch along fold-line to hold layers together.

At stitching line, press side hem away from lining. Press side edges to wrong side at side hemlines over again to make a double hem.

# Tape Headings

Self-styling tapes in a variety of shirring styles and widths make customizing window treatments easy. Curtains can be made even more unique through the selection of rod styles. The height of the curtain will depend upon the hardware chosen. Follow manufacturer's recommendations for determining fullness and length.

## MATERIALS

Figure yardage needed for your specific window, (see Determining Yardages, page 25).
■ Fabric
■ Self-styling drapery tape
■ Drapery weights (optional)
■ Hardware, including rods and clips, hooks or pins
■ Fabric glue

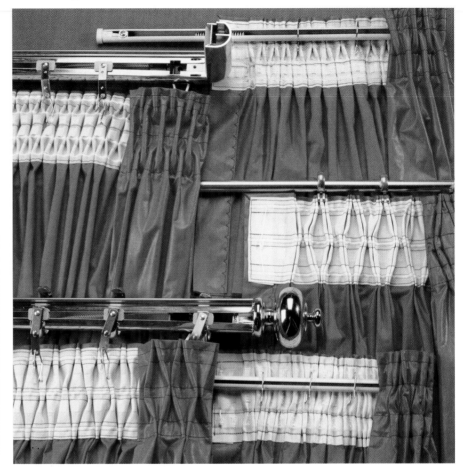

Beautifully styled headings with pleats, smocking, or shirring give your draperies a professional finish. They can cover rods or hang below them, depending on the rod style.

## MEASURING AND CUTTING

Determine finished length and width for curtain. Add for a double hem at the lower edge (see Determining Length, page 26) and 1" (2.5 cm) for a hem at the top. Add double side hems and seam allowances to the width measurement. Cut tape 2" (5 cm) longer than finished curtain width.

## ASSEMBLY

Finish side and bottom hems. Press 1" (2.5 cm) to wrong side at top edge, making a miter at each outside top corner. On wrong side of tape, press 1¼" (3.2 cm) under at

each end, pulling out cords to front side. Pin tape to wrong side of curtain, beginning ¼" (6 mm) from outside curtain edge and ⅜" (1 cm) from top of curtain. Stitch tape in place following manufacturer's instructions. Secure heading to a work surface, marked for distance of curtain width. Tie off cording at one end, and working in 24" (61 cm) sections at a time, adjust pleats. Work from one end and then the other. Tie off cords at each end when fully gathered. Adjust if necessary. Place a pin through the

cording. Wrap a knot around pin and secure it with a dab of fabric glue. Attach excess cording inside heading with a safety pin or square knot and trim ends.

To add a lining with self-styling tape, adjust lining length to run below curtain top finished edge with a 1" (2.5 cm) hem pressed to the wrong side. Place folded top edge of curtain over lining top edge and stitch through all thicknesses to secure tape.

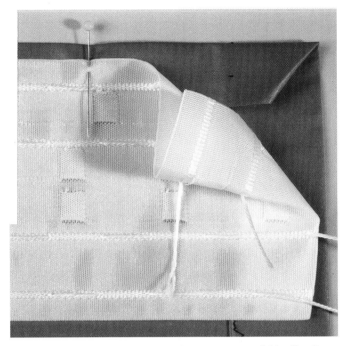

After pressing curtain single hem and mitering corner, fold self-styling tape end under and pin in place with cords pulled to the right side.

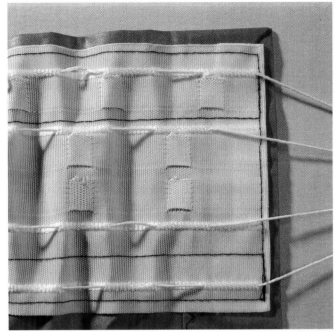

Pin heading to a flat work surface. Tie cords at one end and pull evenly from the other end, adjusting pleats or gathers.

## TIPS

• Match the weight of your fabric to the type of tape used, keeping small gathers for lightweight fabrics and larger pleats for heavyweight fabrics.

• To make sure the tape you select is suitable for your fabric, buy and experiment with short yardages of both. Check to see the fullness of the folds created by the tape as well as the shirred pattern is effective.

• Use jerking motions to draw cords through tape, making sure all tapes are even.

• Adding weights will accentuate the pleat shapes and draw draperies down; eliminating weights will allow draperies to puddle and flow.

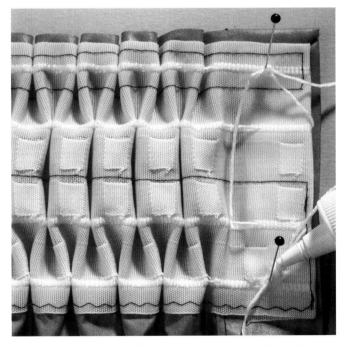

Tie two cords together, pin through knot and secure with glue. Leave ends long so tape can be unpleated if necessary.

# Draped Scarf

Double-tassel braid trim highlights the graceful fall of the scarf edges. Contrast lining also would set it off. This is one of the easiest and most versatile window treatments to sew with a pattern (see page 126).

Composed basically of a lined panel of fabric with diagonally cut ends, a scarf offers infinite decorating possibilities. It can be made in any size, symmetrical or asymmetrical, with each side falling gracefully to a window mullion, sash, sill or to the floor. Allover prints and solids are best fabric selections since they can be "railroaded" into one piece. Solids are elegant when decorative trim is added to the inner edge.

## MATERIALS

- Fabric and lining fabric 54" (137 cm) wide
- Swag holders or tiebacks
- Tassel fringe
- Self-adhesive hook and loop tape
- Fabric glue
- Fusible tape, if desired

## CUTTING

Position swag holders or tiebacks, at the outside upper corners of the window molding. Measure width between swag holders and add length from swag holders to desired finishing point on either side. Add 1" (2.5 cm) for seam allowances. Measurements are for a scarf with the back edge straight across the top of the window. If you want the scarf to drape more, adjust to a longer length.

Cut desired length and place drapery and lining fabrics with right sides together. Trim selvages from both edges. To create angled end for cascading pleats, lay fabric lengthwise on surface. Mark front edge from one short end as follows: For short scarf, mark 19" (48.5 cm) from end; for sash-length scarf, mark 29" (73.5 cm) from end. Lengthen this measurement if you want more lining to show. Fold fabric along an imaginary line con-

necting the mark and the back corner on the same end. Smooth fabric and press along fold. Open out and cut along fold.

## ASSEMBLY

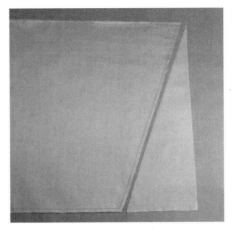

With right sides together, stitch around all four sides of scarf with ½" (2.5 cm) seam, leaving a 12" (30.5 cm) opening in the center of the longest side. Trim corners, turn right side out and press. Slipstitch opening closed, or fuse seam allowances together with fusible tape, if desired.

To cut other end to match, fold fabric layers in half crosswise, matching upper corners. Repeat angle cut and open out fabric.

## FINISHING

To apply double row of tassels, layer tasseled braids on top of one another with tassels alternating. To add stability, glue trim before hand-sewing to ends and shortest edge. Hand-sew or machine-stitch to scarf edge through all layers.

To create even draping, lay scarf on a large flat surface and fan-fold evenly across width every 6" (15 cm). Place a band of extra scrap fabric around the folds to hold them in place temporarily.

# Swag Holders and Tiebacks

Swag holders and tiebacks come in many decorative styles and shapes, including tassels and rings. Make sure tieback complements your fabric and drapery style.

## ROSETTES

For each rosette, cut two bias fabric strips 7" (18 cm) wide by 80" (203 cm) long, piecing if necessary. With wrong sides together, fold strip in half lengthwise. Starting from raw edges, mark and cut a 45 degree angle at each end of strip. With wrong sides together, serge or machine-stitch raw edges together with 1/4" (6 mm) seam allowances.

To gather rosette, stitch 3/8" (1 cm) from raw edges. Use ruffling technique of zigzag stitching over carpet thread or cord (see Chapter 1, Ruffling Techniques). Secure cord at one end and gather rosette tightly. Secure threads at ends.

Beginning at one end, roll gathered fabric to form rosette. Thread milliner's needle with gathering thread and hand-sew rolled edges tightly together as you roll. Attach rosette to swag holder with glue or self-adhesive hook and loop tape.

Attach a strip of self-adhesive hook tape to upper edge of holdback. Lay folded scarf over holdback, adjust drape and drop, and attach loop tape to scarf to hold it in position.

# Swag and Jabots

A traditional toile fabric with contrasting lining makes the most of the classic lines of a swag and jabots. The following instructions, along with a purchased pattern (see page 126), will help you to make and mount this window treatment.

# Swag

Once considered a very formal window treatment, swags and jabots are now equally at home in the country and the city, depending upon the fabric you select. A zigzagging shape at either end that is easily pleated is the secret of a successful swag.

### TIP

A solid or nondirectional fabric lends itself to being cut on the bias to fall into soft folds. Fold fabric on the diagonal and place pattern's foldline on the diagonal fold. While this will require more yardage, it makes graceful folds and is recommended for long swags and other applications.

### MATERIALS

**Covered Mounting Board**
- Board, 2" (5 cm) wide by 1" (2.5 cm) thick by width of swag
- Lining fabric to wrap swag board
- Angle brackets to attach boards
- Screws
- Staples and staple gun

**Swag and Jabots**
- Fabric
- Lining fabric
- Fusible tape
- Purchased pattern
- Covered mounting board

### CUTTING

Refer to the pattern measurement chart to determine pattern view and pattern pieces to fit your window. Estimate width by deciding first where you will mount the swag. In this project the treatment is mounted on a fabric-covered board to maintain a crisp clean line at the top edge. See techniques for Mounting Boards, page 45.

Fabrics with motifs that provide mirror images or with a motif that can be centered, nondirectional prints, and solids all take easily to the folds of a swag. Check also that the fabric drapes nicely.

Cut drapery fabric using pattern piece. Cut lining piece slightly larger than pattern piece. With right sides together, place drapery fabric swag piece over lining and trim lining to match on bottom edge only. To make a band to finish swag top, cut drapery fabric 4" (10 cm) by swag width plus 1" (2.5 cm) for seams.

### ASSEMBLY

With right sides together, stitch fabric and lining together with a ½" (1.3 cm) seam along lower curved edge. Trim seam allowance to ¼" (6 mm). Turn right side out. With lining side facing up, roll drapery fabric forward toward lining, "favoring" so that about ⅛" (3 mm) of drapery is to lining side and press along edge, pushing iron toward lining. Serged edges will favor almost automatically.

After favoring the lower edge, on right side, press, pin, and machine-baste along the sides and the upper edge.

Trim lining along sides and top to match drapery fabric.

To pleat swag, pin a fold at each inside notch. Working from the bottom up, fold and stack the pinned folds, one on top of the other. Bring creased folds together to align raw edges with swag top. Check that total top width matches measurement of mounting board. If swag is too narrow, loosen between each fold. If swag is too wide, tighten folds.

## SECURING THE SWAG

Bring folds together aligned with swag top. Mark width of mounting board on a flat surface. Adjust measurements if necessary. To make band, press 1/2" (1.3 cm) to wrong side on band ends to match swag length. Press 1/2" (1.3 cm) to inside along one long edge. Press band in half with wrong sides together and open out. With right sides together, pin unpressed band edge to front of swag and stitch using a 1/4" (6 mm) seam allowance.

Fold pressed edge to the back over the seamline. To hold fabric in place and prevent slipping, fuse along banded edge with fusible tape. With swag right side up, stitch in-the-ditch along the seamline through all layers. Stitch pressed ends together.

# Jabots

### CUTTING

Cut left and right jabots and linings. Mirror-match print motifs on drapery fabric from one side to the other if necessary. On the diagonal edge of the lining fabric only, cut an additional 1/4" (6 mm) off to prevent sagging or curling.

### ASSEMBLY

With right sides together and matching diagonal raw edges, pin and stitch only diagonal edges together with a 1/2" (1.3 cm) seam. Trim seam allowance to 1/4" (6 mm). Press seam allowances to wrong side toward lining. Match

remaining raw edges and stitch together with a 1/2" (1.3 cm) seam, leaving top edge open. Trim seam allowance to 1/4" (6 mm). and trim across corners. Turn right side out and press along each side edge. Press again along diagonal, favoring drapery fabric to inside.

Place jabot wrong side up on pressing surface and fold long edge forward, equaling return, and press. With right side up, working from pressed return edge, fold pleats evenly and pin in place, from return edge to inside edge. Hold folds in place with masking tape applied to both front and back.

### MOUNTING

With board mount application, jabots can be applied either over or under the swag. To make the window appear wider, mount jabots first, then swag. To make window appear taller, mount swag first, then jabots over the top. Center board on window, resting on angle irons. Mark position of screw holes on underside of board for ease of mounting later. See Mounting Boards, page 45.

## MOUNTING BOARDS

### MATERIALS

- Board, 2" (5 cm) wide by 1" (2.5 cm) thick by width of window treatment
- Lining fabric to wrap board
- Angle brackets to attach boards
- Screws
- Staples and staple gun

### CUTTING

Cut board to top width of window treatment. To cut lining casing, measure board circumference plus 1" (2.5 cm) for seams for width. Add 2" (5 cm) to board length for lining length.

### ASSEMBLY

Fold lining in half lengthwise and stitch a $^{3}/_{8}$" (1 cm) seam along long edges and one short end. Turn right side out. With seam centered on one short side of board, slide sleeve over board. Fold excess lining over board end, stapling in place and trimming as necessary.

Covered boards should be installed with angle irons beside or directly into the wood frame. Use 1" (2.5 cm) thick boards by width required for installation. For inside mount, cut board $^{1}/_{2}$" (1.3 cm) shorter than inside frame measurement. For outside mount, cut board at least 2" (5 cm) longer than outside frame measurement. Install angle irons next to frame, even with the top of the woodwork. Boards also can be installed above the woodwork.

Make a pilot hole through the fabric and into the board, using an awl, for each screw placement. This will prevent the threads of the fabric from twisting around the screw.

Measure board circumference and length. Make a sleeve casing long enough to cover board ends. Seam lining, turn right side out, and slip board into casing.

Finish mount by folding, mitering, and stapling lining to board end.

Starting from inner corner of the jabot, make equal folds to point where return is marked and pin in place. Machine-baste across jabot top to hold pleats in place. Prepare and apply band in the same manner as for swag band application. Repeat for second jabot.

Place banded edge of swag over board top. Center and staple band to top of mounting board, lining up swag to drop over front board edge. Starting from the return, pin jabot bands in position, making sure they are even. Staple bands to mounting board top, mitering corners. Mount board to angle irons.

# Relaxed Roman Shade

The Roman shade gives a window a finished look without impeding the view. The lambrequin framing the window is softly padded and fabric-wrapped. Though stunning with the lambrequin, the shade is handsome enough to stand on its own.

This charming variation of a Roman shade allows fabric to fall in soft relaxed folds. Start with fabric rectangles and seam them, add decorative tape and rings, and install with hardware. Place your tapes in line with the vertical window mullions on large window installations. From the inside, aligning tapes or rings with mullions minimizes shadows and integrates the design. From the outside, the mullions hide the mechanism of rings and cord. Avoid fabric with print motifs that would interfere with your seam and ring placement. You can pick up colors in the print by accenting the Roman shade with coordinated strips or trim. Decorative strips allow you to turn seams to the shade's front side and cover them instead of having them show through the window.

## CUTTING

Where possible, plan seams so they coincide with vertical mullions in the window. To determine width, add 1" (2.5 cm) for side seams and the same amount for each pieced seam to window opening measurement. Piece as necessary, with wrong sides together and taking into consideration the position of seams in relation to mullions. To determine length, measure height of window and add 5¹/₂" (14 cm) for a 2¹/₂" double hem at the lower edge and ¹/₂" (1.3 cm) for top seam allowance. Cut accent fabric strips same length and 1" to 3" (2.5 cm to 7.5 cm) wide, and allow 1" (2.5 cm) for seam allowances. Cut strips to line up with Roman shade cords or rings and both side seams. Cut a mounting board to fit (see Mounting Boards, page 45).

## ASSEMBLY

With *wrong* sides together, piece panels with ¹/₂" (1.3 cm) seam allowances. Attach rings or tape and accent strips as below. On long strip edges, press ¹/₂" (1.3 cm) to the right side. Following manufacturer's instructions, apply fusible tape to each strip edge, leaving paper backing intact.

To finish lower edge hem, press and stitch in 2¹/₂" (6.5 cm) double hem across the bottom. Attach top to band for mounting board as for swag (see Securing the Swag, page 44 and Mounting Boards, page 45).

### MATERIALS

**Covered Mounting Board**
- Board, 2" (5 cm) wide by 1" (2.5 cm) thick by width of shade
- Lining fabric or poplin
- Screws
- Staples and staple gun

**Roman Shade**
- Shade fabric
- Accent fabric for trim or accent braid
- Plastic rings or Roman shade tape
- Nylon cord
- Eye screws
- Covered mounting board
- Paper-backed fusible tape ¹/₂" (1.3 cm) wide
- Cleat
- Curtain rod (temporary)
- Weighted drapery pull

## ATTACHING RINGS AND TAPE

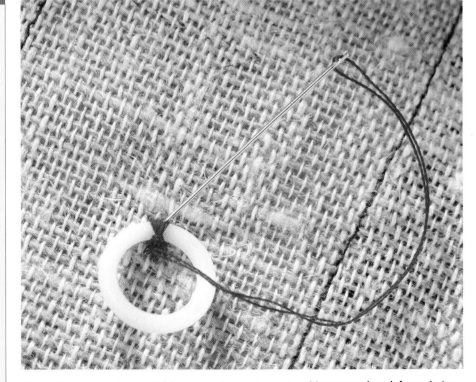

For single rings, apply accent fabric strips first and rings last. Measure and mark for each ring, starting ¹/₂" (1.3 cm) above finished hem edge. Place rings for double folds at regular intervals, from 5" to 10" apart, and in the same position across the shade. Use double thread and hand-tack each ring in place with four stitches, catching the strip of fabric once. Double-knot and trim excess thread.

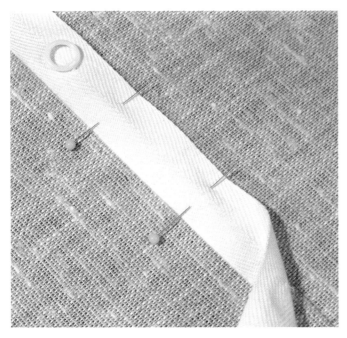

For ring tape, apply tape first and accent fabric strips last. Place fabric wrong side up. Measure 5½" (14 cm) from bottom for ring placement. Leave 1" (2.5 cm) of tape extending below ring. Center tape over each seam, pin, and use zipper foot to stitch each edge of ring tape to shade. At sides, measure in 1" (2.5 cm) from side edge, position tape with rings in line with other tapes and stitch along each edge of tape. Cover bottom edge of tape with turned hem.

Press ½" (1.3 cm) seam allowance to wrong side on long edge of each strip and open out. Following manufacturer's instructions, apply fusible tape to right side of seam allowances. Remove paper from fusible tape and fold seam allowances to wrong side along pressed lines. Center over seams and ring lines and fuse in place. With zipper foot or edgestitch foot, edgestitch along both edges.

## FINISHING SHADE SIDES

To finish shade sides, matching raw edges, stitch right side of fabric strip seam allowance to wrong side of shade seam allowance ½" (1.3 cm) from raw edges.

At side edges, press fabric strip and seam allowance to front of shade. Press along seam edge to set in place, fusing remaining strip edge to front and edgestitch with a zipper foot or edgestitch foot.

After stitching shade top to band and stapling band to mounting board top, assemble Roman shade pull-up system. Anchor eye screws into bottom of board to match the rows of rings. Beginning at shade bottom, knot cording on ring and glue knot to secure. Thread cord through rings above, through eye screw and over to one side. Repeat for all rows so that all cords are run through top rings and rest on one shade side. For ease of installation, place a rod temporarily in bottom hem.

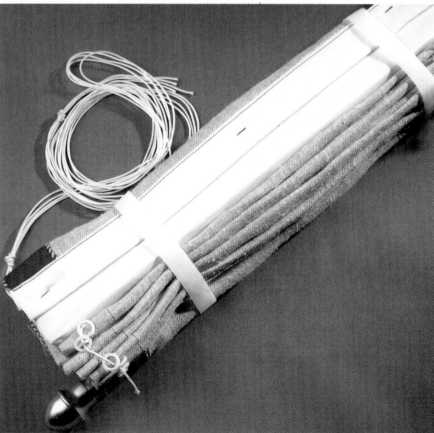

Pull all cords tight to distribute folds evenly across shade. Hold shade in position with fabric bands. Screw mounting board to inside window frame (see Mounting Boards, page 45). Release bands. Let shade down. Adjust cords for equal tension. Hold cords together and knot, securing with glue, just outside last eye screw. Thread cords through weighted drapery pull, 18" (46 cm) beyond first knot, knot cords again, cut off excess cords. Attach cleat to window frame and wind cords around cleat to hold shade in place.

# Shaped Valance

This swag- and jabot-window treatment, in a graceful curved flat pelmet shape, can be altered with a centered pleat to cover double windows. Jabots take on a bell curve that drapes on a curtain pole. This unique variation is from a purchased pattern designed by Susanna Stratton-Norris (see page 126).

# Shaped Valance

Choose the same fabric for lining and accent band as shown, or use coordinates. Use fabrics of the same weight and construction for best results.

## MATERIALS

- Purchased pattern
- Curtain fabric
- Band and lining fabric
- Wood pole, finials and brackets
- 1/4" (6 mm) paper-backed fusible tape

## CUTTING

To make center pleat on double window version, use all pattern pieces for that version plus the center piece 4 from View B. To adjust piece 4, remove $2^3/8$" (6 cm) from the entire center fold edge and add 1" (2.5 cm) to the top of the extended section with the notch. Cut a band for piece 4, the same width as the other band pattern pieces, following the lower edge shape of piece 4. Cut another piece 10 to go over the rod.

Make the swag with the center section, following the directions for swag B center section and pleat according to swag B finishing directions. Remember to add the center section band to the band for swag C. Then follow the band directions for swag C. Finish center section by attaching piece 10 according to directions for swag C. Finish ends of double swag with jabot following pattern directions.

## ASSEMBLY

Install curtain pole, approximately 3" (7.5 cm) above window frame with brackets aligned with outside frame edges, making sure curtain will fit within brackets. Treat the double window as one span.

For swag, center pattern over print motif before cutting to size, matching print motifs for all swags. With right sides together, press and pin swag front over lining and cut lining to size.

For jabots, center motifs similarly on each, including new center piece.

To assemble, follow pattern directions except apply paper-backed fusible tape to right of upper band seam allowance before stitching in place. When assembling, press band seam allowances toward lining and press band edge, favoring the band side as for Swag, page 42.

For lining, either use the pattern piece or try this technique for an even truer lining fit: With right sides together, press curtain fabric over coordinated lining fabric. Pin around all edges, press and then cut.

After pressing upper band seam allowance to the inside, fuse ¼" (6 mm) paper-backed fusible tape to the same seam allowance, easing around curves. Do not remove paper.

Press seam allowances at lower edge toward lining. Press fabric band to front of the curtain, favoring band edge. Remove paper from fusible tape and fuse fabric band in position.

# Box-Pleated Valance

An elegant box-pleated valance lends distinction to any curtain or drapery treatment. Board mounting assures that it stays staunch and crisp. Make the valance traditional as shown, formal with a rich fabric and edge-trimming such as damask and silken braid, or country casual in buffalo plaids.

## MATERIALS

### Covered Mounting Board
- Board, 2" (5 cm) wide by 1" (2.5 cm) thick by width of valance
- Lining fabric
- Angle brackets
- Screws
- Staples and staple gun

### Box-Pleated Valance
- Drapery fabric
- Lining
- Covered mounting board

## CUTTING

Determine placement of significant print motifs in relationship to pleats in designing the valance; choose a fabric that lends itself to this treatment. Make valance wide enough and deep enough to clear draperies. Generally, the best scale relationship is valances $1/8$ the length of draperies. Determine length needed and add 5" (12.5 cm) for bottom hem and top finishing. Cut lining fabric 4" (10 cm) shorter than decorator fabric. To determine width, plan pleat placement. Each box pleat requires 12" (30.5 cm) of additional fabric. Add 1" (2.5 cm) for each seam allowance and for side seams. Measure width, including returns, and add seam allowances and 12" (30.5 cm) for each pleat.

## ASSEMBLY

With right sides together, stitch raw edges of drapery fabric panels together with a $1/2$" (1.3 cm) seam. Stitch lining panels together to match seams of drapery fabric, or "railroad" fabric. With right sides together, align bottom raw edges of lining and drapery fabric and stitch together 2" (5 cm) from raw edge. Press double hem and lining toward the wrong side of drapery fabric. Matching raw edges along sides and top, stitch using $1/2$" (1.3 cm) seam allowances, along each raw side edge. Trim corners and turn right side out. Match raw edges of fabric and lining across the top. Press side and bottom edges.

## FINISHING

With right sides together after stitching lower edges, align top edge of drapery fabric and lining and hand-press 2" (5 cm) double hem to the bottom. Stitch each side edge closed, and trim corners. Turn to right side and zigzag or serge top edges together.

See Mounting Boards, page 45. Measure and mark for pleats (top row in photo). Mark center of pleats and 6" (15 cm) to each side. With right sides together, join markings and stitch 2" (5 cm) vertically from top edge to prevent pleats from gapping (bottom). Machine-baste pleats in place $1/2$" (1.3 cm) from top edge. Place top of valance 1" (2.5 cm) over board edge and staple into position.

# CHAPTER 3

# Pillows Plus

Pillows are the signature that give a room individuality. They add comfort for both the body and the eye, and the smart home decorator knows how to make use of them to bring together diverse textures, patterns, and styles. Use pillows to experiment with different fabrics and color schemes and to coordinate with other design elements in a room. Pillow covers can be made in many different shapes and sizes, with a selection of closures and details, creating almost limitless possibilities. Instructions for an assortment of pillow covers appear on the following pages.

# Pillow Basics

The projects in this chapter include highlights of procedures used to create beautiful pillows, including special details such as ruffles, cording, and braid. Several closure methods are also explained.

## Fabric

Before choosing fabric for your pillow cover, consider the final use of the pillow. If the pillow is for purely decorative purposes, by all means use the finest, most elaborate or delicate fabrics and expensive braids or trims, and don't worry about laundering. However, if the pillow will find its home in an active family room where it will be used under sleepy heads for naps or hugged when a teddy is not available, sturdiness of fabric and ease of care are most important considerations. Most pillows will fall between these two extremes.

However, not every fabric design will work as a pillow. If your fabric has a distinct design motif, make sure it can be attractively displayed on the pillow front. For example, a large floral pattern will traditionally be centered on the pillow, with the remaining fabric or contrasting fabric used to create a ruffle, covered cording, or decorative trim.

A very large motif may not fit at all. A more creative approach may be to place half the design on each of a pair of knife edge pillows, so that when they are placed together, they form one large design. Be sure you have sufficient fabric to carry out your design ideas.

Smaller print designs can be made more distinctive by highlighting them with a contrasting fabric border, similar to a mat framing a print.

## Closures

A closure allows easy removal of the pillow cover for laundering or a seasonal decorating change.

The overlapped or French back closure is the simplest. It doesn't require any extra notions and the finish is smooth. In some applications the back might gap, but this can be alleviated with hand-sewn bar tacks.

Snap tape and hook-and-loop closures have more visible stitching and are suitable for heavy fabrics. These closures can be cut to any length, are very sturdy, are unlikely to malfunction, and will last the life of the pillow.

Button closures add a tailored finish and may become a design element of the pillow cover. They are particularly effective on crisp, lightweight fabrics, and, on the front side, are a perfect showcase for exquisite buttons, such as antique collectibles, natural wooden buttons, or modern button covers.

Zippers are easy to apply and use and are relatively inconspicuous. They are a sturdy closure, and the one most likely to maintain the shape of the pillow.

If you don't want the closure to be visible at all, try a "hidden" band closure. While generally used in conjunction with a zipper, the covering band can be used to cover any type of closure. It can also be embellished to become another design element.

## Pillow Forms

Pillow forms are available in an ever-increasing variety of materials and sizes. The most widely used stuffing is polyester fiberfill. Also popular, especially with those preferring natural fillers, are down and feathers, as well as woollen fleece. Foam forms are usually molded into shape and are perfectly formed. If you find them a little stiff, wrap them in a layer of batting before placing inside pillow.

Fiberfill comes in a range of densities, shapes, and sizes, as well as qualities. It is allergy free and requires less "plumping" than down or feather pillows. You will find it available in square, round, oblong, cylinder and heart shapes.

Sizes range from 10" (25.5 cm) rounds to 30" (76 cm) square floor pillows. Fiberfill is graded either standard or superior quality. The superior fill has greater "loft," meaning it is fluffier, softer, and bounces back more quickly. Superior fill pillow forms generally have fabric covers that are likely to last longer than the non-woven covers on standard pillow forms. Both types are machine-washable.

Fiberfill will not deteriorate, crumble, or mat with age. If you are planning to make pillows in a finished size not commercially available, you can buy fiberfill by the bag, make a cover from muslin and stuff it to create your own pillow insert.

## MAKING A SIMPLE PILLOW

The untrimmed knife-edge pillow is the basic building block in pillow construction. Master this simple pillow and everything else will fall into place.

### CORNERS

A square pillow with pointed corners is best when adding tassels. For other trims, rounded or tapered corners create a more graceful line. Cut two squares $1/2$" (1.3 cm) larger than the desired finished pillow size in both length and width. To alter the corners, fold pillow front into quarters, matching raw edges and corners. Measure and pin 4" (10 cm) from each side of corners through all layers. Mark a rounded corner using a plate or saucer as a template. For a tapered corner, mark $1/2$" (1.3 cm) in diagonally from corner. Draw lines connecting pins to corner marking. Trim excess fabric through all layers.

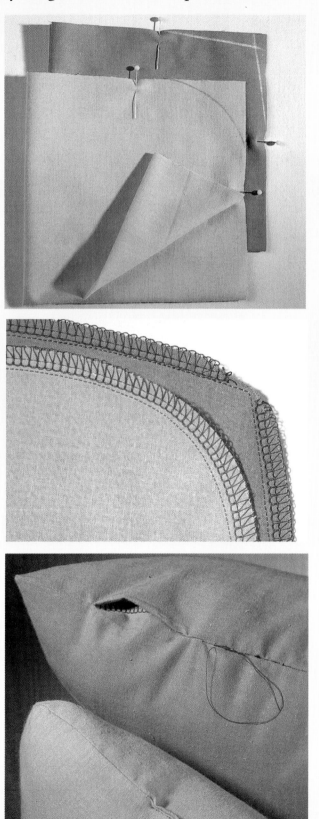

### ASSEMBLY

For altered corners, trim corners of pillow back to match front. Unfold pillow front and place on pillow back with right sides together and raw edges even. Pin, placing pins perpendicular to edge so they can be stitched over. Mark an opening on one side of the pillow front 2" (5 cm) in from each corner. Stitch the pillow front to the back with a $1/4$" (6 mm) seam allowance, securing threads at beginning and end of marked opening. Zigzag or serge around edges. For tapered corners, trim diagonally across corner as shown.

### FINISHING

Turn pillow right side out and press, creating a knife edge. Press opening seam allowances to the inside. Stuff pillow or insert pillow form, folding form slightly to slip through opening. To close opening, slipstitch pressed edges together. Or, you can also pin openings together and machine-stitch as close as possible to the pressed edge.

# Pillow Closures

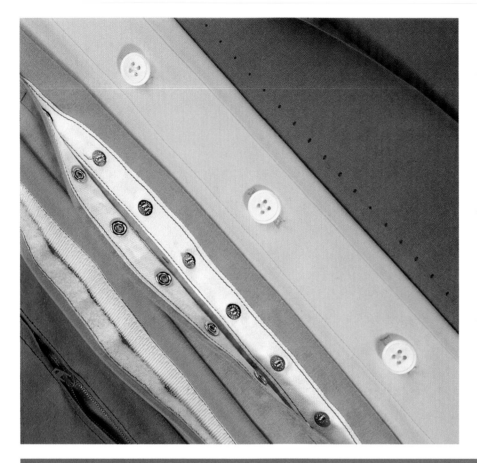

The simple pillow is sewn closed at the seam. You may prefer to use a closure that allows you to sew smoothly around all four sides of the cover and enables it to be removed easily. We recommend most closures be placed 3" (7.5 cm) above the lower edge of the pillow back. This allows sewing ease while creating an inconspicuous closure. Prepare the pillow front with the desired corner treatment. After completing the closure, trim the back to match the front.

## Overlapped or French Back

This is the simplest closure, requiring no additional notions, and it creates a cover that is very easy to remove. For most pillows, use an overlap of 3" (7.5 cm). For large pillows, overlap 5" (12.5 cm) and adjust the cutting measurements.

Cut pillow back 7" (18 cm) longer than pillow front. Measure 6" (15 cm) up from lower edge and cut across width of fabric. Zigzag or serge over closure edges if necessary. On closure edge of larger back piece, press 3" (7.5 cm) to the wrong side. Blind-hem or straight-stitch in place. On smaller piece, make a 1" (2.5 cm) hem in same manner. When pillow cover is completed, press and insert pillow form. You may wish to add bar tacks (see page 61, right) to prevent the closure from gapping open.

With right sides together, layer larger piece over pillow top, matching raw edges. Place smaller piece on top, overlapping hems. Pin and stitch together around all sides. Clip corners and turn right side out through back opening.

# Bar Tacks

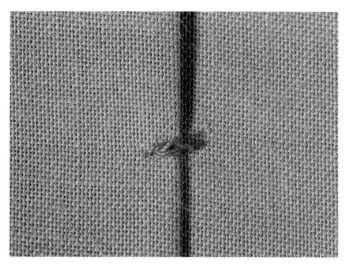

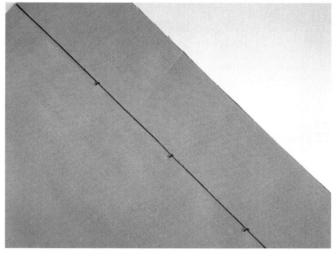

Thread needle with double strand of thread and knot ends together. Conceal knot inside opening and take 3 or 4 stitches across folded edge of overlap into underlap. To finish, insert needle inside pressed hem edge and exit 1" (2.5 cm) past bar tack. Clip off thread at point of exit.

Place bar tacks at 3" (7.5 cm) intervals along closure. To remove the cover for cleaning, snip through the bar tacks and pull the threads out. After cleaning, replace the pillow cover and make new bar tacks in the same position as before.

# Tape Closures

Both snap tape and hook-and-loop tape closures require the same insertion technique. Use tape ³/₄" (2 cm) wide and 3" (7.5 cm) shorter than the finished pillow width. Cut pillow back 3" (7.5 cm) longer than pillow top. Measure 4¹/₂" (11.5 cm) from lower edge of pillow back and cut across width of fabric. Zigzag or serge over closure edges.

On closure edge of larger back piece, press 1¹/₂" (3.8 cm) to wrong side and open out flat. On right side,

center tape, socket side up, across width and ¹/₄" (6 mm) from pressed edge. Stitch around all four sides of tape. Fold overlap to wrong side along pressed edge. Stitch again along one long edge of tape through both fabric layers.

On right side of smaller back piece, center tape, ball side up, across width and ¹/₄" (6 mm) from outside edge of closure, taking care to align sockets with ball sections. Stitch in place as for socket sections.

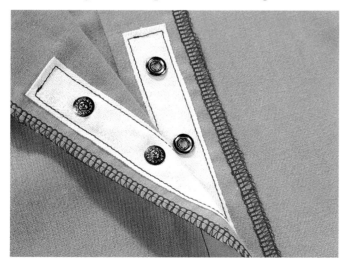

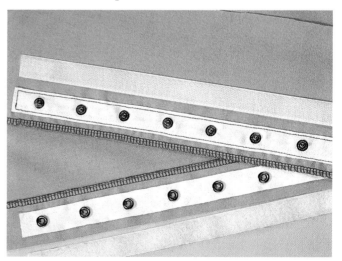

Close pillow back. With right sides together, pin front and back together and stitch around all sides. Open closure and turn pillow right side out.

Follow the same steps when applying hook-and-loop tape, placing loop (soft) side in same position as socket side of snap tape. Stitch or glue in place and topstitch.

# Button Closure

Button closures add fresh, tailored appeal to pillow covers. Cut pillow back 7½" (19 cm) longer than pillow front. Measure 7½" (19 cm) up from lower edge and cut across width of fabric. Press 1½" (3.8 cm) to wrong side twice along each closure edge. Blind-hem or straight-stitch in place. Measure and mark larger back piece for buttonholes, spacing them evenly about 3" (7.5 cm) apart. Make buttonholes ⅛" (3 mm) larger than diameter of buttons. Sew buttons to right side of smaller back piece to correspond with buttonholes.

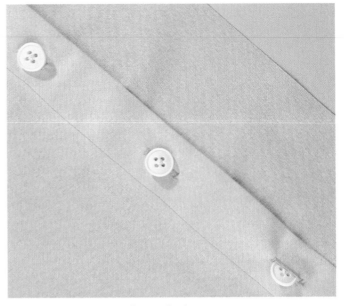

Button back pieces. Stitch front to back.

# Zipper Closure

Zippers are readily available in a variety of colors and lengths, and are a popular choice for pillow closures. Cut pillow back 2" (5 cm) longer than pillow front. Measure 4" (10 cm) from lower edge of pillow back and cut across width of fabric. Zigzag or serge over closure edges. Purchase zipper 3" (7.5 cm) shorter than the finished pillow width. Mark zipper position 1½" (3.8 cm) in from each edge.

With 1" (2.5 cm) seam allowance and right sides together, stitch closure edges together between markings and ends, securing threads. Baste between markings. Press seam open, and following manufacturer's instructions for lapped zipper application, stitch zipper in place.

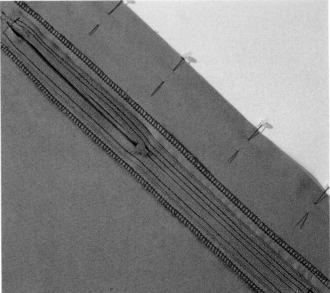

Open zipper before stitching front and back together. Pin front and back with right sides together and stitch. Turn pillow right side out through zipper opening.

# Hidden Closure

While a band closure is generally used over a zipper, it can be used to hide all other closures as well. We have personalized the band with decorative machine stitching and contrasting thread, but many other decorative possibilities exist. Try using a 3" (7.5 cm) wide piece of contrasting or matching ribbon, or a band of contrasting fabric. Bands may be wider, but should not be narrower than 3" (7.5 cm). If inserting a zipper beneath the band, use the centered zipper application so the zipper will lie flat. Cut pillow back 2" (5 cm) longer than pillow front. Press in half and cut across width. Insert zipper following zipper closure instructions, left (page 62).

To make the band, cut a strip of fabric 7" (18 cm) wide by the width of the pillow front. Fold strip in half lengthwise with right sides together and stitch along longest edge with 1/4" (6 mm) seam allowances to make a tube.

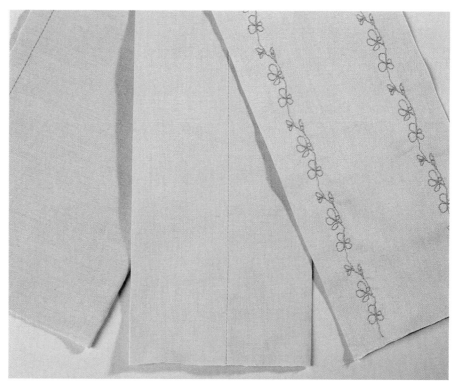

Turn right side out and press tube flat with seam in center of one side. If desired, work a row of decorative stitching 1/2" (1.3 cm) from each edge of front.

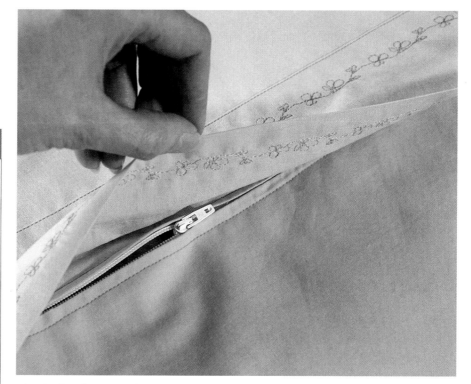

Place back with zipper right side up. Zipper should be slightly open. Place band with seam centered over zipper. Baste short ends of band in place. Edgestitch along one long edge of band. Place front and back with right sides together. Pin and stitch around all sides, trim, and turn pillow cover right side out through zipper opening beneath band.

## TIPS

• Edge the hidden closure band with ruffles or pregathered eyelet. Stitch narrow ribbon to the edge.

• Another decorative option is to pleat the band. Start in the center and fold pleats, working out to either edge, with pleats facing toward each edge.

• Stitching options for bands include pin tucking, quilting, smocking, and cording. Try other machine embellishments such as preprogrammed embroidery motifs or monograms.

# Fabric Accents

Whether it's one pillow or many, fabric choice determines the overall effect. An eclectic grouping of pillows is far more interesting when coordinated fabrics are used for mock welting, gathered welting, and ruffles.

# Mock Welting

A mock-welted edge is an easy way to add a designer look to your pillows. The effect is like that of a pillow with self-welting. Large welting, worked over a thick cable cord, works best.

Cut the pillow front oversized in both length and width to accommodate the wide cable cord to be placed inside. Add twice the diameter of the cable cord: if the cable cord is $1/2$" (1.3 cm) in diameter, add 1" (2.5 cm) around all sides; if 1" (2.5 cm) in diameter, add 2" (5 cm) around all sides.

Round or taper corners following instructions in Making a Simple Pillow (page 59). Cut pillow back to fit pillow front. Finish pillow back with desired closure. Stitch pillow front to back with right sides together, turn right side out. Press seam edges flat.

## TIPS

• Mock welting looks best in nondirectional prints and solids. You can further embellish it with grosgrain ribbon at the seamline.

• To make a gathered mock welted edge, leave a 3" (7.5 cm) opening at center of the lower pillow edge when stitching cable cord in place. Pull cord out from each end, distributing gathers around the pillow edges to desired fullness. Usually, removing $1/5$ of cable cord is ideal. Trim the cord and sew or glue ends together. Press the cord into the opening and top-stitch closed.

• Mock welting looks best in nondirectional prints and solids. You can further embellish it with grosgrain ribbon at the stitchline.

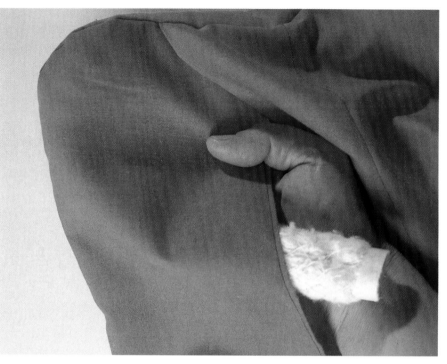

Fit a length of cable cord inside perimeter of pillow butted to seamed edges and cut cord to this measurement. Remove cable cord and glue or sew cord ends together to prevent raveling.

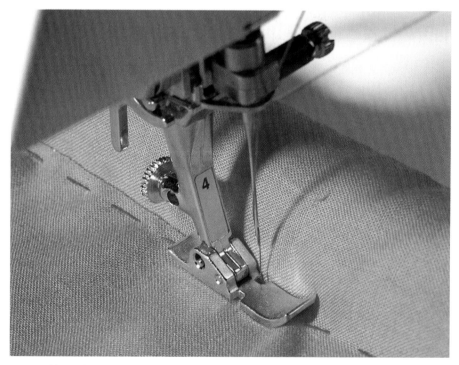

Insert cable cord through closure, with cord ends at center of lower edge. With fingers, press cord tightly against seamed edges. To prevent seamed edges from rolling or shifting out of position, hand-baste next to inner edge of cable cord. With zipper foot, starting at center of lower pillow edge, stitch next to inner edge of cord, stitching as close to cord as possible. Remove basting stitches and insert pillow.

# Gathered Welting

Gathered welting, especially in a contrasting fabric, adds elegance to your pillows. See Chapter 1, Welting Techniques, for how to make gathered welting. Cut out pillow front and taper or round corners (see Making a Simple Pillow, page 59). On right side of pillow front, mark center of lower edge. Pin gathered welting in place, matching raw edges. Use ³/₈" (1 cm) seam allowances and begin stitching welting 2" (5 cm) from center mark. Trim the cord and sew or glue ends together. Join welting ends as instructed in Chapter 1. Finish pillow back with desired closure and complete.

Stitch gathers in place, using a zipper foot and adjusting the gathers evenly with your fingers.

# Adding Ruffles

Adding ruffles can soften the look of a pillow. See Chapter 1, Ruffling Techniques for how to make ruffles. Pillow ruffles are generally two to three times the perimeter of the pillow, with less ruffles for heavyweight fabrics. Add extra ruffling to crowd into corners to maintain fullness. A folded ruffle is an ideal choice for a pillow because it leaves no stitched edges or wrong sides of fabric showing. Cut out pillow front, adding ³/₈" (1 cm) seam allowance, and round or taper corners following instructions in Making a Simple Pillow (page 59). Finish pillow back with desired closure. Set back aside.

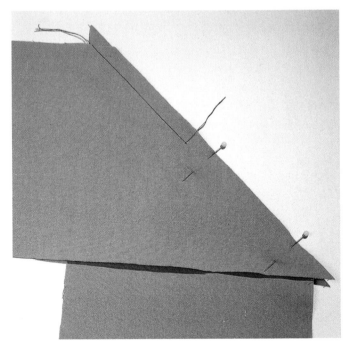

For a double ruffle, join strips, right sides together, with a diagonal ¹/₄" (6 mm) seam and press flat. With wrong sides together, press ruffle strip in half lengthwise, matching raw edges.

Make gathering stitches, starting and ending at markings, using ruffler attachment or desired gathering method. Divide ruffle into four equal sections and pin-mark. On right side of pillow front, match pins to each corner. Pull gathering threads up at each corner to fit side. Pin in place.

Stitch ruffle to pillow front with $^3/_8$" (1 cm) seam allowance. With pillow front and back right sides together and ruffles sandwiched between, pin raw edges together.

## TIPS

• When gathering, use a strong pin or small-gauge crochet hook to distribute gathers evenly aross each side, allowing extra fabric at corners.

• Wrap excess cording or thread around corner pins to secure.

• Distributing gathers evenly is much easier when you have a large, flat surface to push pins into. Lay pillow top right side up, match and pin ruffles to corners and secure with push pins for adjusting ruffles along each side.

• To eliminate added bulk created by ruffling, trim entire seam allowance to $^1/_4$" (6 mm) after stitching to pillow front.

• Add additional color with a double ruffle. Make two ruffles, the front $^1/_2$" (1.3 cm) shorter than the back ruffle. Use pregathered lace as an alternative to fabric. Gather and stitch as one.

• Mix and match pillows by alternating ruffle and pillow fabrics for a coordinated group of pillows.

• Add trim to the edge of the ruffle. Stitch or fuse ribbon, pregathered lace, rattail, or decorative braids.

With right sides together and front on top, stitch around pillow with a $^3/_8$" (1 cm) seam allowance, stitching just inside ruffling stitching line. Keep edges even and remove pins as you stitch. Straight-stitch or serge around pillow again with a $^1/_2$" (1.3 cm) seam allowance.

# Trim Accents

Trims, braids, fringes, and tassels add a distinctive lushness to pillows. One of our most popular home decorating designers is Bebe Winkler. You'll find the following information helpful when you purchase the pattern for her collection of elegant pillows (see page 126).

## Elegant Trims

Opulent trims and rich braids take pillows to a new dimension. Combine many trims or use one as the sole accent.

Following are instructions for edging a pillow with brush fringe; making an envelope trim; edging a pillow with twisted braid; and combining twisted braid and ruffling, shown clockwise from bottom right corner.

## Brush Fringe Trim

Sometimes called moss trim, brush trim is available multicolored or in solid hues. Fringe is secured by stitching the heading into the side seam of the pillow.

Cut front and back of pillow, adding a ¹/₂" (1.3 cm) seam allowance, and round or taper corners following instructions in Making a Simple Pillow (see page 59). Finish pillow back with desired closure. Pin brush fringe to right side of pillow front, with fringe toward pillow center and matching heading top to raw edges. If fringe is flat or sparse, crowd extra heading and fringe at corners for added fullness. Stitch in place.

Place pillow front and back right sides together, and stitch a ¹/₂" (1.3 cm) seam around all sides. Turn the pillow right side out.

Secure fringe with masking or transparent tape to keep it from getting caught in the seam. With a zipper foot, baste in place along lower edge of fringe heading.

# Twisted Braid

Braid with an attached heading tape is easily stitched into the seam at the edge of a pillow. Finishing and joining the ends can be tricky, but is easy. Cut pillow front and back and finish back with desired closure. Mark center of lower edge of pillow back.

With fabric glue, attach twisted braid, matching edge of tape with raw edges, and beginning 2" (5 cm) from center mark. End 2" (5 cm) from center point on opposite side, and allow 3" (7.5 cm) extra at each end of tape. Begin stitching 1" (2.5 cm) from center mark, and stitch braid in place, ending 1" (2.5 cm) before center mark. Clip tape at corners if necessary.

Measure pillow perimeter and cut braid 6" (15 cm) longer for overlapping and weaving.

On the left side, pull strands and secure under the heading tape, twisting back into the original braid shape. Secure with transparent tape or pins. Twist strands together and baste in place along the heading tape in same direction as the braid twists. Trim cords 1/2" (1.3 cm) from basting stitch and flatten along the seam allowance.

Securely stitch braid ends in place. With right sides together, stitch pillow back to front using a zipper foot to crowd as close as possible to braid. Turn pillow over and stitch from front side again, crowding stitches as close as possible so braid is flush with pillow seam. Turn pillow cover right side out.

Adding tassels to pillow corners is easy. Pin or tack a tassel in each corner with cord across the seamline and strands toward center. Secure strands with masking tape. Stitch cord in place when stitching the seam.

Clip stitches between braid and heading tape at each end. Separate braid cords and wrap each strand end with transparent tape to prevent raveling. Trim heading tape, leaving a 1" (2.5 cm) overlap and secure ends with a pin or transparent tape.

Twist and pull strands at right over strands at left until they appear to be one continuous twisted braid. Secure right strands with transparent tape across header tape.

# Braided and Ruffled Trim

Ruffles add softness while braid adds its own defining elegance. Generally make ruffle at least two times the width of the braid. An off-seam closure is necessary to keep hems smooth and even.

Stitch braid to pillow front as for Twisted Braid. Follow instructions for adding ruffles (page 66), then pin ruffle to heading tape, matching raw edges. Baste ³/₈" (1 cm) from edge. Pin pillow front and back together. After stitching once, turn pillow over and stitch again, crowding stitching at seamline. Trim edges and turn pillow right side out.

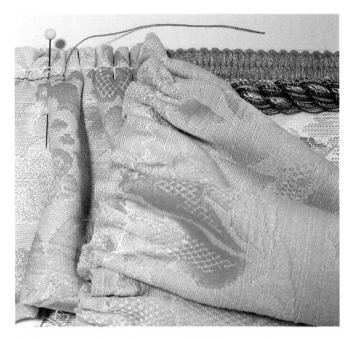

With zipper foot, stitch ruffle in place ¹/₂" (1.3 cm) from the edge through all layers.

# Envelope Trim with Fringe

Pin or use fabric glue to hold braid right side up, with fringe toward raw edge. Pin mitered corners and stitch inside braid edge. Flip fringe back over decorative braid toward pillow center and secure with masking or transparant tape. With right sides together, stitch pillow back and front with a ³/₈" (1 cm) seam allowance. Turn pillow cover right side out.

Cut pillow front and finish pillow back with desired closure. Determine desired size of envelope flap and use a disappearing marker to mark the center point, and lines extending to two top pillow corners. Measure and cut flat braid to fit along marked line. On right side, pin center of braid and place over marked line, matching centers and mitering at point. Apply a small amount of fabric glue to hold turned point of braid in place and continue adding dabs of glue 1" (2.5 cm) apart along marked lines. Starting at the point and stitching to the corners, topstitch both sides of braid with invisible or matching thread.

To add fringed braid to outer edges of pillow, on the pillow front, mark a line in from the pillow edge equal to the fringe header depth with disappearing marker. Cut braid to measurement, adding 2" (5 cm) for adjusting corners and ends. Pin braid in place, finger-pressing and pinning miters at corners. Final corner will have half-miter piece covering first end of braid. Loosely hand-tack along outer edge if desired.

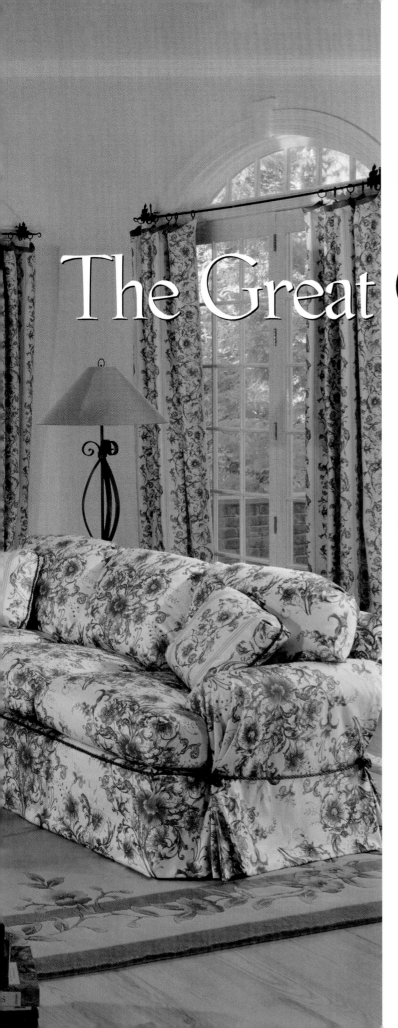

# CHAPTER 4

# The Great Cover-up

Cover-ups give seating a quick change and a new look that will magically transform a room. Whether you want to refurbish existing furniture or make a seasonal decorating change, the options are limitless. You will find it takes minimal effort to wrap and tie upholstered sofas and chairs or to give straight-back chairs new life with cushions or covers. Ordinary folding chairs can be transformed with Cinderella slipcovers. Even outdoor furniture gains stature with made-to-match cushions. Once you master box cushions, you can add or replace seating for hard chairs or soft sofas . . . the technique is the same.

# Covering Basics

Cover-ups add custom-made charm while setting the mood for casual style. In most cases only simple sewing is required, so any of these cover-ups makes a great first-time project.

## Fabric

Choose fabrics in solid colors or with an allover design so matching prints will not pose a difficulty. When selecting prints, choose short repeats. Make sure that one-way designs or fabrics with a nap will work for your chosen cover-up. You simply may need to purchase extra fabric for one-way layouts. For some projects or patterns directional motifs are unsuitable. Consider fabrics with built-in stain protection, easy laundering properties or both. Preshrink fabric if necessary.

Large size fabrics such as sheets make ideal cover-ups because you can avoid seams. However, you may want to give sheets added heft and support by quilting them to a muslin backing or having them professionally quilted. For upholstery, fabrics of medium weight are preferred, even for cover-ups.

Conversely, consider using extremely heavy fabrics for cover-ups but make sure that the fabric will lend itself to graceful gathering or folding where needed. Blanket cloths, primitive rugs and heavy muslins or linens all make sensational cover-ups with gathers appropriately compressed. Test small samples for malleability before you purchase all yardage.

## Color

If covering large pieces, select colors you love to see daily for a permanent cover-up, or plan on more than one cover-up set and choose colors to set the mood for the season. Remember they will have a lot of impact in a room. White, off-white, blue, and green are fresh colors for welcoming summer; deep reds and plums are an antidote to the chills of winter. Neutrals have either a warm or cool base and, depending on which you choose, can be dressed up with removable accessory trims that will create a similar effect.

## Purchased Sewing Patterns

Ready-made patterns are available with instructions for slipcovering many different sizes and shapes of sofas and chairs. Since exact fit is not essential to the beauty of most covers, the patterns can be modified to suit your seating, no matter how unique. This planned inexactness carries over to the construction of these covers. You do not need to be a fine seamstress to create these wonderful looks. The final effect often is helped by a casual, open-minded approach to sewing. It is the overall look that is important.

## Fleece

Fusible fleece adds a soft roundness to edges and provides light padding for comfort — and good looks — to seats and chair backs, and it can add bulk to fine or inexpensive fabrics. Follow manufacturer's instructions for use.

Plain fleece or batting can be used most effectively to pad out arms, backs, and seats of upholstered pieces. Use as many layers as necessary and tack it in place before covering so that it won't "travel" or bunch up.

## Trimmings

Whether you are updating your interior or making a seasonal switch, look for the extras that will give your work a more finished and professional look. Buttons, both purchased and self-covered, braids, ribbons, and trims all will add to the new look you want to achieve.

Don't be hesitant when purchasing trims. If you can't decide between two sizes of braid or welting, go with the larger. When deciding on the number of rows of buttons, go ahead and add that extra one. Instead of adding a single tassel, add a group of them, and make bows bigger rather than smaller.

# It's a Wrap

Change the look of upholstered sofas and chairs by simply wrapping, tucking, and tying. If you prefer to follow a pattern, refer to the pattern listing (see page 126). Otherwise, follow these steps to loosely fit your own tie-on slip cover.

# Slipper Chair Cover-up

For a slipper chair, start covering by draping fabric on platform and skirt sections first. Fabric should extend at least 1" (2.5 cm) on floor. Adjust fullness at corners so fabric drapes evenly. With a disappearing fabric marker, draw a hemline around fabric where it meets the floor. Trim fabric 1" (2.5 cm) beyond hemline. Press 1/2" (1.3 cm) to wrong side twice for hem and stitch close to the pressed edge.

Repeat for the back section, draping first to the platform in front, then to the floor in back. Drape corners and finish hem same as for front.

Mark sides and corners of draped fabric where it meets the floor to establish the hemline, then mark it.

## MATERIALS

- Decorator fabric
- Coordinating fabric for a reversible cushion cover, if desired
- Decorative twisted braid
- Twill tape for drawstring
- T-pins

**You will need approximately:**
- For a chair without arms, 5 to 6 yds. (4.6 m to 5.5 m).
- For a chair with arms, 6 to 8 yds. (5.5 m to 7.35 m).
- For a loveseat, 10 to 12 yds. (9.15 m to 11 m).
- For a sofa, 16 to 20 yds. (14.65 m to 18.3 m).
- For each cushion, an additional 1 to 1 1/2 yds. (.95 m to 1.4 m).
- Purchase additional yardage for matching prints.

### ESTIMATING YARDAGE

Measure sofa/chair in the following sections: deck platform; skirt front and sides; chair top, front and back; cushion top, sides, and bottom. For sofas and chairs with arms, also measure arm and side section. Add 3" (7.5 cm) for seam allowances and hems on all edges.

### CUTTING AND FITTING

With a disappearing fabric marker, mark each section on right side of fabric, indicating fabric direction (up) with an arrow. *Make sure any print direction is correct for each piece.* If piecing, cut two panels, each the measurement of the cutting length. Cut one panel in half lengthwise and stitch one half to either side of the full panel.

# Wrapped Seat Cushion

Measure across the top and down both sides of the cushion in both directions and add 12" (30.5 cm). Cut two pieces of fabric to measurements, rounding corners. With right sides together, stitch a seam 1/2" (1.3 cm) from edge, leaving a 6" (15 cm) opening. Turn right side out. To make a drawstring casing, stitch 1/2" (1.3 cm) inside finished edge, leaving a 3" (7.5 cm) opening.

For a non-reversible cover, cut one thickness to the same size, finish cut edges with a serger or zigzag. Press 1/2" (1.3 cm) to wrong side and stitch in place for casing. Insert drawstring.

Cut a twill tape drawstring slightly larger than the circumference of the cushion and attach a safety pin to one end. Insert safety pin and draw string through opening.

Place seat cushion over fabric and pull up drawstring, adjusting fullness around cushion. Arrange most gathers at corners and finger-press to soften. Tie and tuck under cover.

# Covering Arms

**Platform and skirt front:** Cut fabric to length measurement and width of the platform, plus height of skirt, plus 3" (7.5 cm). Press and stitch a ¹/₂" (1.3 cm) double hem on skirt edge and platform edge. Position platform and skirt section with hemmed edge even with floor and fabric extending evenly at corners. Fit skirt fabric around arm, beginning at inner arm of platform and working to outside on the floor. Allow 3" (7.5 cm) for tucking under platform and back, folding edges and pinning in place. If necessary, miter deck/skirt fabric, forming a point at the corners.

**Back:** Drape fabric over back and front to platform allowing 1" (2.5 cm) for hem at floor and with fullness draping evenly at lower corners. Add 3" (7.5 cm) for tucking on inside of platform. Adjust fullness at corners. Beginning at platform and working up, with disappearing marker draw a stitching line on fabric along each existing arm seam. Cut fabric 2" (5 cm) beyond marking, continuing down each side to floor. Clip curves.

**Arm and side sections:** Drape fabric evenly at corners, extending 1" (2.5 cm) on floor. With disappearing marker, mark hemline. Beginning at platform and working up, draw a stitching line on fabric along each existing arm seam, ending at corner. Leave a 2" (5 cm) seam allowance and cut on seam allowance. Continue down side, clipping as needed to fit, taking care not to cut into back section.

## ASSEMBLY AND HEMMING

Remove back, side, and arm sections from sofa or chair. With right sides together, pin arm and side sections together at back. Match stitching lines and hemlines, and stitch together. Adjust fit if necessary. Trim 1" (2.5 cm) beyond hemline. Press ¹/₂" (1.3 cm) to wrong side twice and stitch in place close to folded edge. Place cover on furniture and tuck in excess fabric at platform.

## Finishing

Make folds along back, arms and corners of slipcover and hold in place with T-pins. For corners, place the pins under planned braid position, at least 1" (2.5 cm) below the edge of the deck. Beginning and ending at center back, wrap braid around gathered fabric at corners. Make a double knot in the braid at center of each gathered corner. Finish at center back with a decorative knot.

Tack graceful gathers at corners with T-pins and hold in position with knotted twisted braid. Use T-pins to hold braid in place.

As a decorative option, twist two different colors of braid together and wrap as one. Select colors from the fabric print for a harmonious effect.

# Folding Chair Covers

Transform an ordinary folding chair into a star. Consider making sets of covers in the same fabric or in contrasting fabrics to mix and match as needed.

Hold pattern tissue in place and compare its shape with the shape of the chair. Adjust pattern tissue length and width to fit the shape of your chair. If shape differs, mark a new stitching line. If necessary, adjust chair seat. Remove pattern from chair and draw a second line 1/2" (1.3 cm) beyond any new lines for seam allowance. Connect new lines with original cutting and seamline. Construct chair cover according to pattern directions.

Use fusible fleece to pad chair seat and back for slight cushioning and to stabilize and add weight to lightweight fabrics. Cut fleece 1/2" (1.3 cm) smaller than seat and back pattern. After stitching the cover, fuse fleece to wrong side, following manufacturer's instructions.

This and other variations are easy to make from a purchased pattern (see page 126).

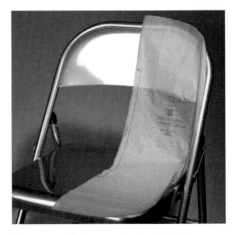

Place pattern tissue on chair with foldline centered on chair.

## FITTING

To hem cover, place cover over chair and use masking tape to hold pleats in place. With a fabric marker, draw a hemline around lower edge, even with floor. Cut hem to 1" (2.5 cm) beyond line. Press ½" (1.3 cm) to wrong side twice and stitch close to pressed edge.

To secure cover to chair, cut two pieces of twill tape each 20" (51 cm) long. Fold pieces in half and tack fold to seam allowances at side of chair. Tie cover to chair around leg.

## FINISHING

As a decorative option, use twisted braid to tie a double bow, then tack a large tassel to the end. Or purchase a tasseled drapery tieback and make a bow, inserting doubled braid back through holder.

Center braid bow on back of chair and tack in place. For easy removal, attach with hook-and-loop fastener.

# Customizing Chair Covers

Adding distinctive trimmings to chair covers is an ideal way to express personal style. Piping, ribbon, cording, tassels, braids, buttons, ruffles, and other decorative touches add a custom finish to chair covers. Select trims that enhance the fabric you have chosen and the mood of your room. Always check care instructions for compatibility with fabric or attach trims in such a way that they can be easily removed prior to laundering if necessary.

Purchase novelty buttons or cover your own with matching or contrasting fabric. This chair cover can be made with a purchased pattern (see page 126).

## Button Accents

When making self-covered buttons, dampen fabric before cutting. When fabric dries it will shrink slightly and create a tight fit around the button cover. Plan button position on chair cover. Mark with a permanent marker. Insert button safety pin through fabric, then through button shank and back through to the wrong side of the fabric. Remove buttons for laundering, replace with pins at marks.

To reposition or remove buttons from chair cover for easy care, attach buttons with button safety pins.

# Soft and Pretty

Straight-backed chairs do not need to be hard-edged and modern. By selecting a full-skirted chair cover and embellishing it with piping and other trim, you can transform a wallflower into the belle of the garden party. Get as fancy as you like using any or all of these ready-made trims.

**Preruffled edging** is available in several widths or finishes, hemmed, or with a decorative edging. It can be stitched into a seam, under a hem, or be combined with other trims.

**Pregathered ruffles** can be purchased flat, lightly stuffed with fiberfill, or with inner cording for a dimensional effect.

**Piping** is stitched into a seam to accent an edge and can be custom-made or purchased to match or coordinate.

**Ribbon** is available in a selection of colors, widths, and finishes. Use ribbons to trim, tie, or border an item.

Various ready-made trims to consider include, top to bottom, preruffled edging, pregathered ruffles, piping, and ribbon.

Even the simplest piping makes this chair cover something special. This and other variations are easy to make from a purchased pattern (see page 126).

# Cushion Cover with Ribbon Ties

For added richness, combine several layers of ribbon. Cut two lengths of ³/₄" (20 mm) wide grosgrain ribbon to fit lower edge of chair skirt with a 1" (2.5 cm) overlap. Place ribbon strips beside each other. Cut a piece of contrasting ribbon the same length and center it over the two ribbons. Glue or fuse top ribbon in place with fusible webbing creating a three-piece ribbon. Stitch along long edges of center ribbon to secure. Pin ribbon trim to sides and front of chair cover, beginning at a back corner. Topstitch close to upper edge of ribbon, turning ends under and stitching in place. Stitch another length of ribbon along back flap.

Use ribbons in place of the traditional fabric ties shown above or when bias binding is suggested. This and other variations can be made from a purchased pattern (see page 126).

To tie cover to chair, cut two more lengths of ribbons but do not join. Fold in half and tack at back corners of chair cover. Slip cover onto chair and tie ribbon into bow around chair post. Trim ribbon ends and apply seam sealant to prevent fraying.

# Chaise Lounge Cover

Cushions will add comfort and appeal to even inexpensive patio furniture, making it useful both indoors and out. Adapt the instructions for other extended seating. For more seating options, consider a purchased pattern (see page 126).

## MATERIALS

- Purchased pattern
- 2¹/₄ yds. (2.1 m) decorator fabric
- 8³/₄ yds. (8 m) high loft batting
- 5³/₈ yds.(5 m) piping
- ⁵/₈ yd. (.6 m) of 1" (2.5 cm) wide elastic
- 15 self-covered buttons ³/₄" (20 mm) in diameter
- 15 buttons ³/₄" (20 mm) in diameter
- 6" (15 cm) hook-and-loop fastener 1" (25 mm) wide
- Upholstery needle and thread

## STRAPS

## CUTTING

If necessary, adjust pattern tissue to fit chaise. Hold tissue in place and compare finished cushion size. Adjust stitching and cutting lines if necessary. Cut out from decorator fabric, following pattern instructions.

To make strap for back of cushion to hold cover in place on chaise, make casing for elastic. Cut elastic 21" (53.5 cm) long and insert into casing. Baste across ends. Position at markings and baste in place close to upper edge of back section.

## TABS

To make tabs for cushion, cut fabric 2¹/₂" (6.5 cm) wide and long enough to wrap around chaise back leg and bottom of frame at side, plus ¹/₂" (1.3 cm) for seam allowances. Press ¹/₄" (6 mm) to wrong side along all cut edges. Press tab in half lengthwise, with wrong sides together. Topstitch close to all edges.

Cut hook-and-loop fastener for each tab and stitch opposite sides of fastener to opposite sides of tab. Fold tab in half crosswise. Pin to back section of cover at pattern markings.

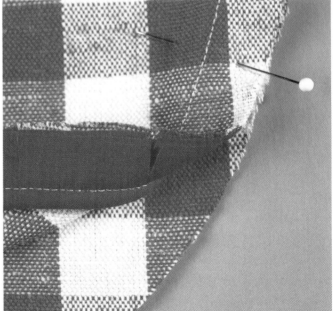

Baste piping to front. Pin front and back sections together over tabs and elastic casing. Clip seams at corners. Stitch over piping basting, leaving an opening for turning.

Turn cover to right side and press. Close tabs.

## STUFFING

To stuff cover, cut batting following pattern. Trim seam allowances. Cut batting into three lengthwise sections following pattern markings: upper, center, and lower. Insert upper batting section into cover and stitch across marked line through all layers. Insert remaining sections of batting, lower section first, and stitch across cover as before.

## ADDING BUTTONS

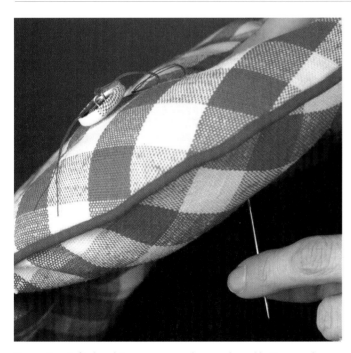

To create a tufted cushion, use covered or purchased buttons and thread a long upholstery needle with heavy-duty thread. Tie ends of thread to shank of button, leaving a 4" (10 cm) tail. Insert needle through cushion and pull tight. Thread needle through a second button and bring it tight against bottom of cushion.

Wrap thread around button shank to secure. Tie off thread ends securely under top button. Trim thread ends.

# Be Seated

Our lineup of cushions includes a box cushion with piping, box cushion, and mock box cushion. Box cushions create a tailored look. Add piping to define the shape even further, in contrasting or matching colors for a classic, traditional look in seating. For more contemporary seating, try the mock box cushion, which is also the easiest to do.

## Mock Box Cushion

### MATERIALS

- Decorator fabric
- Zipper to fit back edge of cushion

The seams on this pillow are halfway around the sides instead of a band. Corners are clipped to square off the cushion cover.

Measure cushion side to side across top, plus halfway down each side and add 1" (2.5 cm) for seam allowances. In the opposite direction, measure from front to back across cushion top and halfway down front and back. Add 1½" (3.8 cm) seam allowances. Cut two matching pieces of fabric, one each for top and bottom.

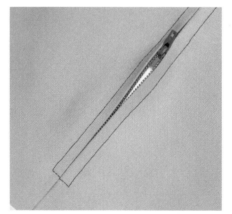

With right sides together, pin back edge of cushion sections and baste, using 1" (2.5 cm) seam allowance. Press seam open and insert zipper following manufacturer's instructions for centered zipper application. Open zipper partially. Seam ½" (1.3 cm) around raw edges.

To miter a corner, press seam open. Separate layers, then fold to match seams. Center seams and pin. Measure the side depth of the cushion. At right angles to the seam, draw a line the same length of this measurement with a fabric marker. If pillow depth is 4" (10 cm), the line should be 4" (10 cm) across. Stitch along line, trim close to stitching. Turn cushion right side out and press. Insert cushion through zipper opening.

# Box Cushion

## MATERIALS

- Decorator fabric
- Zipper 4" (10 cm) longer than back edge of cushion
- Piping twice the perimeter of the cushion (optional)

Cut cushion top and bottom 1" (2. 5 cm) larger than the finished cushion. Pin back boxing strips together along one long edge. Baste 1" (2.5 cm) from one long edge. Press seam open and insert zipper, following manufacturer's instructions for centered application. To stitch boxing, place on cushion top, centering zipper on one edge and extending around each side.

Cut one boxing strip the length of the front and both sides, less 1½" (3.8 cm), by the finished boxing height plus 1" (2.5 cm) for seam allowances. For back boxing strips, cut two strips the back edge length measurement plus 5½" (14 cm), by half the boxing height plus 1½" (3.8 cm) for seam allowances.

Mark corner position on both edges of boxing strip. At corner point, clip strip almost to stitching line. Pin one long edge of strip to top with right sides together. Stitch in place with ½" (1.3 cm) seam allowance. Stitch cushion bottom in place in same manner. Turn cushion right side out and press. Insert cushion.

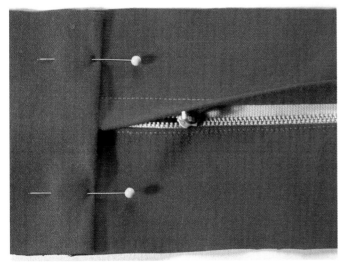

Press 1" (2. 5 cm) to wrong side on one short end of long boxing strip. Lap end over remaining strip to cover zipper tab, with cut edges even. Pin in place. Stitch through all thicknesses ½" (1.3 cm) from fold. Using a ½" (1.3 cm) seam allowance, stitch remaining short ends of strip with right sides together at bottom of zipper. Open zipper.

To add piping, stitch to right side of top and bottom pieces, clipping at corners and at each side of corner to ease welting. If cushion is difficult to insert into cover, wrap a piece of plastic over cushion to slide it into cover. Be sure to remove plastic.

# CHAPTER 5

# Dressing the Table

Making your own tablecloths and accessories provides a perfect way to tie together an existing decorating scheme, to change the mood of a room, or to begin the shift to a new range of colors. Reversible table covers and toppers provide options for using the same coverings in a variety of combinations to create a quick change. If your table is an odd size, your custom-made coverings will provide flawless fit. Depending on your personal style, make your table coverings and napkins simple or embellish them by adding decorative trims, borders, fringes, and braids.

# Place Mats and Runners

Breathe new life into your dining area with mix-and-match place mats, table runners, and accessories. Make runners and place mats from your favorite fabric, or use two coordinating fabrics for added impact. A thin layer of batting, lightweight interfacing, or fusible fleece between fabrics will add protection for your table finish and extra body to the fabric. Use fringe, binding, or a border as the final flourish.

# Fringed Runner, Place Mats, and Napkins

Add color and texture to every table you set. All you need to create lush fringed edges is a loosely woven fabric and a little patience. This technique requires almost no sewing at all.

## MATERIALS

- Loosely woven decorator fabric in cotton, linen, or blends

## CUTTING

Cut runner at least 12" (30.5 cm) wide and at least 12" (30.5 cm) more than the length of your table. Cut four 18" (46 cm) square napkins. Cut four place mats each 12" x 18" (30.5 cm x 46 cm). *Take care to cut on the straight grain of the fabric.* To establish straight grain, pull a thread ¹/₂" (1.3 cm) from the raw end of a length of fabric. Cut along the pulled thread.

## RUNNER

Finish long edges of runner with a narrow hem. To mark for fringe depth, measure 4" (10 cm) from cut edges and pull a thread across fabric. With either a straight stitch or narrow zigzag, stitch above pulled thread. Use a flatlock stitch on a serger as a decorative option. Stitching will prevent further fraying during use or laundering. To fringe fabric, unravel threads below and parallel to the stitching line. Knot fringe every ¹/₂" (1.3 cm) or use the woven fabric design as a guide.

## NAPKINS

Cut napkins 18" (46 cm) square on the straight grain. To fringe fabric, pull a thread ¹/₂" (1.3 cm) from cut edges. Straight-stitch or zigzag above the pulled thread. Unravel threads below and parallel to the stitching line.

## PLACE MATS

Make placemats in same manner, fringing as for runner or napkins.

## TIPS

- If using a multicolored check fabric, to keep the end fringe in a single color, stitch along the raw ends of any turned hems to prevent raveling before turning. Trim reverse side fringe at stitching line, leaving only one color at corners.
- For a multicolored fringe, use two contrasting fabrics and make a reversible runner. Leave colors mingled or knot each color separately.
- For a double-knotted fringe, lengthen the amount of fringe. Divide each knotted fringe in half and knot again. Add more knots if desired.

# Bound Place Mats

An oval place mat finished with bias binding is an attractive and easy-to-do choice. The binding can be made from the same fabric, a contrasting fabric, a coordinating fabric used elsewhere in the room, or it can be purchased in a matching or contrasting color. To cut your own bias tape, see Chapter 1, Cutting Continuous Bias Strips on page 17.

## MATERIALS

- Place mat fabric
- Backing fabric
- Batting, fusible fleece, or lightweight interfacing
- 1" (2.5 cm) wide bias binding strips cut from coordinating fabric **or** purchased bias binding
- Bias tape maker or bias binding foot (if desired)

## CUTTING

Cut 4 rectangles each 12" x 18" (30.5 cm x 46 cm) from place mat fabric, backing fabric and batting, fusible fleece, or interfacing. Round off corners using a dinner plate as a marking guide. Cut binding 1" (2.5 cm) longer than circumference of place mat.

## ASSEMBLY

Sandwich batting between place mat and backing fabric with raw edges even. Follow manufacturer's instructions to apply interfacing or fleece to wrong side of backing fabric. Baste around cut edges through all layers. Make a strip of continuous bias binding, see Cutting Continuous Bias Strips, page 21, or use purchased bias binding. Attach bias tape. To help ease binding around curved edges, shape binding to match place mat with a steam iron. If your machine has a bias binder, use it to shape, bind and stitch the binding simultaneously.

## BINDING

Unfold one side of bias binding and pin right side to back of place mat with raw edges even. Stitch binding in place along foldline. Fold binding to top side of place mat, encasing raw edges and pin in place. Topstitch binding close to pressed edge, ending 1" (2.5 cm) from end.

To finish end, turn under ½" (1.3 cm) diagonally. Lap binding over beginning and continue stitching to end.

# Bordered Place Mats

Set your table in style with inviting one-of-a-kind place mats. Choose one print fabric for the place mat center and a complementary print for the border, and you can use a third coordinate for the backing.

## MATERIALS

- Place mat front and back fabric
- Border fabric
- Batting, interfacing or fusible fleece

## CUTTING

To make place mats finished size 16" x 20" (40.5 cm x 51 cm), cut eight rectangles 17" x 21" (43 cm x 53.5 cm) from place mat front/back fabric. Cut one layer of batting, interfacing or fusible fleece for each place mat. Cut border strip $4^{1}/_{2}$" x 80" (11.5 cm x 203 cm).

## ASSEMBLY

Sandwich batting between place mat front and back with raw edges even. Follow manufacturer's instructions to apply interfacing or fleece to wrong side of back fabric. Baste around cut edges through all layers. Press $^{1}/_{2}$" (1.3 cm) to wrong side along one long edge of border strip. With $^{1}/_{2}$" (1.3 cm) extending, pin unpressed edge of border to wrong side of place mat. Cut through border at corner so $^{1}/_{2}$" (1.3 cm) extends past place mat corner. Stitch in place, beginning and ending $^{1}/_{2}$" (1.3 cm) from corner and using $^{1}/_{2}$" (1.3 cm) seam allowances. Repeat for all four sides.

To miter, fold all border ends back diagonally and press. Open out and stitch miters together along diagonal creases.

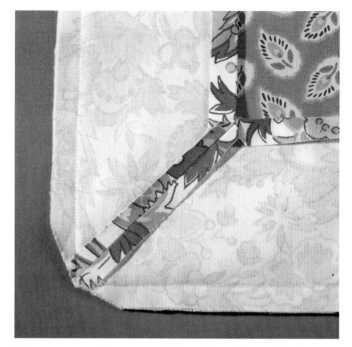

Trim corner seam allowance to $^{1}/_{4}$" (6 mm) from diagonal stitching line. Trim across corners. Press diagonal seam open. Trim remaining seam allowances to $^{1}/_{4}$" (6 mm). Complete corner stitching.

Fold border to top side of place mat, encasing seam; press. Topstitch border close to pressed edge and backstitch for reversible place mat.

# Banded Table Runner

Use this runner instead of a place mat or layer it over a contrasting tablecloth. Runners are made like place mats but are cut the length of the table with an added drop. Use two coordinating fabrics, one for the front and a second for the back and band. For this runner, the decorative fabric used on the back side wraps to the front to form the band. Choose an attractive motif that will work as a border.

## MATERIALS

- Runner fabric (small print)
- One piece back and self-band fabric (large print with stripe)

## CUTTING

Cut one front panel 9" x 60" (23 cm x 185 cm). Cut back 17" x 60" (23 cm x 185 cm). A 12" x 60" (30.5 cm x 152 cm) runner with 2¹/₂" (6.5 cm) wide bands can be cut from ¹/₂ yd. (.5 m) each of two 60" (152 cm) wide fabrics. You will need extra fabric for lengthwise stripes.

## ASSEMBLY

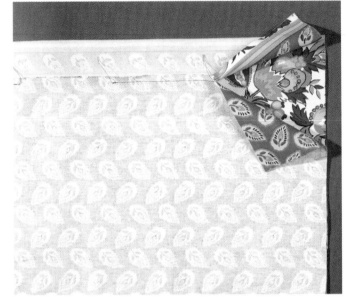

With right sides together, stitch remaining lengthwise edges together with a ¹/₂" (1.3 cm) seam. Press seams toward side edges, centering top panel.

With right sides together and matching raw edges, stitch front and one lengthwise edge of back together with a ¹/₂" (1.3 cm) seam. Leave a 6" (15 cm) opening for turning 12" (30.5 cm) from one end.

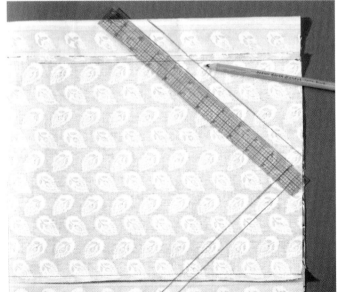

To finish ends of runner, fold runner in half lengthwise and mark center of short end with a pin. Mark ¹/₂" (1.3 cm) in from center. Along each long edge, mark 8" (20.5 cm) from the end. With a ruler and marker, connect edge markings with center marking for stitching line. Mark lines ¹/₂" (1.3 cm) beyond for cutting line. Stitch ends along stitching line and trim excess along cutting line. Turn runner right side out through opening and slipstitch opening closed.

# Custom Napkins

Here's a golden idea! Turn your table into a glittering, star-studded event with elegantly embroidered napkins trimmed in gold and scattered with stars. Complete the look with coordinating place mats and accessories. You'll soon discover napkins offer many embellishment possibilities.

# Scalloped Trim Napkins

## MATERIALS

- 1 yd. (1 m) of cotton or linen fabric to make four 17" (43 cm) square napkins
- Metallic or decorative machine embroidery thread
- Stabilizer
- Seam sealant
- Small sharp-pointed scissors

## CUTTING

Cut four napkins 18" (46 cm) square. Round corners.

## ASSEMBLY

Use metallic thread, scallop-stitch design and satin-stitch length. Attach machine embroidery foot for increased visibility. Wind bobbin with metallic thread at a medium speed to keep thread from stretching. Set your machine for elongated scallops if it has the capability. Test scallops on scrap fabric before sewing napkin.

## DECORATIVE OPTIONS

- Make oversized napkins for buffet service or outdoor dining. Increase finished size to 20" x 20" (51 cm x 51 cm).
- Make kitchen towels into napkins by squaring them up. Use the scrap material for napkin ties. Mix and match various colors and patterns, such as checks, stripes, and prints.
- Make reversible napkins from bandannas by placing wrong sides together and serging or zigzagging the edges.
- Create your own cutwork effects by appliquéing motifs on napkin corners, then serge-finishing around motifs. Serge around inside areas to be cut away and cut close to serging.
- Make modern monograms in miniprints. Cut out block letters, appliqué to napkins, and serge over edges.
- Add tucks, military braid, or decorative stitching in various colors, from napkin edges to 1" (2.5 cm) from edges. Use tones of the same color or select colors to match your favorite tablecloth.

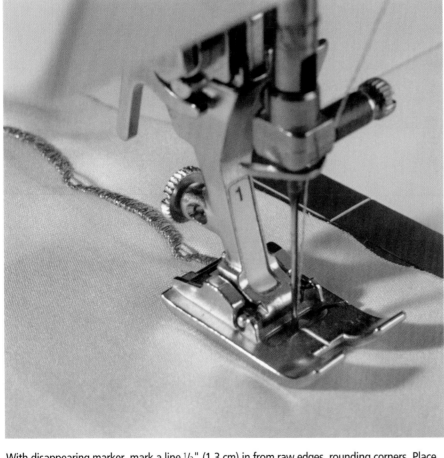

With disappearing marker, mark a line 1/2" (1.3 cm) in from raw edges, rounding corners. Place stabilizer under fabric, or apply liquid stabilizer following manufacturer's instructions. Following machine manual, stitch scallop border along marked lines. Finish edges with seam sealant along edge of stitching, following manufacturer's instructions. Trim fabric carefully beyond scalloped edges with sharp scissors.

# Appliquéd Napkins

## MATERIALS

- 1 yd. (1 m) of napkin fabric to make four 17" (43 cm) square napkins
- Print fabric for appliqué
- Paper-backed fusible web
- Decorative or metallic machine embroidery thread

## CUTTING

Cut four napkins 18" (46 cm) square.

## ASSEMBLY

To serge rolled hem edges, use matching metallic thread in the lower looper and needle. Set serger for narrow rolled-hem stitch, following machine manual. Stitch hem, trimming $1/2$" (1.3 cm) from cut edges. To hem edges with a sewing machine, use metallic thread and a zigzag over edge for a narrow rolled hem.

## TIPS

- Use an embroidery presser foot for best results.
- Always test on scrap fabric before beginning.
- Use a sharp new needle for best results.
- When stitching appliqué, avoid watching the needle. Instead, keep your eyes on the line you are following.
- Stitch twice over the outer edges of the motif; the first row narrow and the second wider for a raised effect.

Prepare appliqué by cutting motif from print fabric, leaving extra fabric around design. Following manufacturer's instructions, fuse paper-backed web to the wrong side of the appliqué area. Trim excess fabric around motif. Peel away paper backing. Place appliqué right side up on napkin fabric and fuse in place. Use decorative thread and satin stitch, setting width in proportion to motif size. Stitch around outer edges of motif, following outline of design.

Don't stop at the stars. Any fabric motif is suitable for this easy appliqué technique. A simple rolled hem is all you need to finish this napkin, or the edge can be corded with your serger.

# Hemstitched Napkins

This classic linen finish is as old as the tradition of the trousseau. Imitate the fine quality of handwork on your sewing machine with a hemstitch needle and a simple zigzag or embroidery stitch. A hemstitch or "wing" needle has flanged sides to make holes between the threads of the fabric that remain after stitching.

---

## MATERIALS

- 1¼ yds. (115 cm) of cotton or linen fabric to make four 17" (43 cm) square napkins
- Metallic or decorative machine embroidery thread
- Wing needle
- Seam sealant

---

## CUTTING

Cut four napkins 19" (48 cm) square for a finished size of 17" (43 cm).

## ASSEMBLY

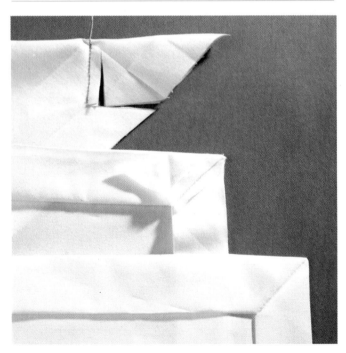

Press 1" (2.5 cm) to wrong side twice along raw edges. Miter corners by opening out pressed edges. Fold corner diagonally with right sides together and raw edges even. Mark from inner corner to fold, forming a triangle within the pressed area. Stitch to inside fold, as shown. With a fabric marker, mark from end of stitching to outer edge and cut along marking. Trim seam to ³/₈" (1 cm). Press seam open. Turn right side out, folding under double hem.

## HEMSTITCHING

Following machine manual, set machine for a zigzag or decorative stitch and insert wing needle and an appliqué or special purpose foot. Select a stitch design that has a reverse motion, one where the needle goes in and out of the same hole more than once, such as decorative three-way stretch stitches. For this application, we used a blanket stitch.

On wrong side, insert needle into fabric next to pressed edge. Stitch, guiding presser foot along pressed edge so that the straight stitch runs next to the fold and the needle swings into the double hem. Pivot at corners, leaving needle down, turning fabric and continuing. Pull threads to wrong side. Use seam sealant to seal thread ends.

---

## DECORATIVE OPTION

To make the remaining hemstitched napkin in the photo on page 95, use a narrow rolled hem to finish the outer edges, stitched with metallic thread on serger or sewing machine. Select a decorative stitch and using wing needle, stitch 1" (2.5 cm) from finished edge, pivoting at corners. We used a cross-stitch design for this technique.

# Reversible Table Ensemble

A skirted table can be tailored to suit a bedroom, living room, kitchen, or dining area. Enhance a basic skirt with decorative trims, such as this twisted braid with heading, to customize your cover, made with a purchased pattern (see page 126).

A well-dressed table adds a personal note to a room. This reversible table skirt and topper will instantly change its look with just a flip of the cloths. Make one side for daily use and the other for more sophisticated formal occasions. While it may only cover a fiberboard table form, the lavishly designed table ensemble is all beauty.

Choose a light-colored fabric for the warm months and a deeper shade for the cooler seasons. Other combinations are created by flipping only the topper or the skirt.

When selecting fabrics for a reversible table cover, be sure they complement each other in color, texture, and weight. Select fabrics that drape well. Before purchasing, drape fabric over your arm or the end cap of a bolt to see if you like the way it drapes. The fabric should have enough weight to hang in folds. It should not be limp, thin, stiff, or unyielding.

When considering trims to finish the lower edge, remember that they must flatter both sides of the skirt as they will be seen whichever side is facing out.

### MATERIALS

- Two coordinating fabrics for reversible table skirt
- Two coordinating fabrics for reversible topper
- Twisted braid with header
- Flat decorative trim with fringe
- Fabric glue
- Matching or transparent nylon thread

## Reversible Table Topper

### MEASURING AND CUTTING

The table topper is a square that drapes over the skirt. Allow a minimum of 6" (15 cm) on each side for drop length; do not allow more than one third of the distance between the table top and the floor. The "points" will drop lower. Topper size is the diameter of table top plus two times the drop length, plus 1" (2.5 cm) seam allowance.

Measure diameter of table top and add drop length plus 1" (2.5 cm). Cut fabric squares for topper and reverse side. Decide on trim placement, considering size of topper and depth of fringe. Using a disappearing marker, mark placement line for top edge of trim. Ours was 5" (12.5 cm) from the edge. Place flat fringed trim along marking, leaving 1" (2.5 cm), extra at each end and corner for mitering.

### ASSEMBLY

With right sides together, pin topper front to back, matching raw edges. Stitch together with 1/2" (1.3 cm) seam allowances, leaving a 10" (25.5 cm) opening for turning on one side. Trim seams and clip across corners. Turn right side out and press. Slipstitch or fuse opening closed along seam.

Pin trim at lower edge of topper, with fringed edge below seam so it will be visible when topper is reversed. Hand-sew trim in place.

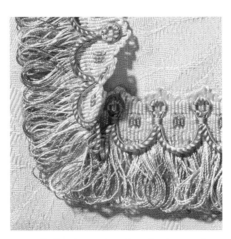

To apply flat decorative trim, glue-baste trim in place at marked line, mitering corners and finger-pressing trim flat.

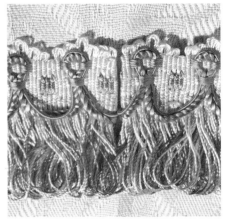

Fold ends under, matching trim design if applicable. Trim ends to 1/4" (6 mm) and pin or glue-baste in place. Topstitch trim to topper along upper edge, using matching or transparent thread.

# Reversible Table Skirt

## MEASURING AND CUTTING

## ASSEMBLY

Stitch fabric panels for each side of skirt with $1/2$" (1.3 cm) seam allowances. For top only, leave a 10" (25.5 cm) opening along long edge of one side for turning. With wrong sides together and matching raw edges, fold fabric into quarters to form a square and to locate the center. Pin all edges together to avoid fabric slipping.

Measure diameter of table top, using a yardstick (meter stick) or metal tape measure. Measure the drop length to the floor. The skirt size is the diameter of the table top plus two times the drop length and 1" (2.5 cm) for seam allowances. For dining, skirt should be no longer than floor length. To enhance the draping of the skirt of an accent table, cut skirt 6" (15 cm) longer than the drop length so that it will puddle gracefully on the floor.

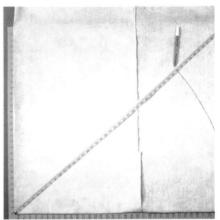

To cut circle, measure the radius (half the total diameter of the skirt), attach a T-pin to the center of the fabric, catching the end of a flexible tape measure. With disappearing marker, mark radius by moving the tape measure in an arc. Cut along marking. Repeat for reverse side of skirt.

### YARDAGE ESTIMATE

- Width or diameter + two times the drop + 1" (2.5 cm) seam allowance = total width of skirt
- Total width ÷ fabric width = number of widths to purchase
- Number of widths x diameter ÷ 36" (100 cm) = total yardage amount

To estimate yardage, divide the total diameter (i.e., table top, 2 drops, seam allowance) by the width of the fabric less 1" (2.5 cm). This will be the number of widths needed. Then multiply the number of widths by the diameter of the tablecloth and divide that amount by 36" (100 cm) to determine the yardage amount.

Since most tables will require more than one fabric width, the skirt and topper will need to be seamed to achieve the finished width. Avoid center seams where possible. Use one full fabric width for the center panel and equal partial panels on each side. Cut center panel the length of the table diameter and two times the drop, plus 1" (2.5 cm). Cut side panels equal widths to measure the total tablecloth diameter plus 1" (2.5 cm). Trim all selvages before joining.

Cut braid to fit circumference of skirt plus 6" (15 cm). Glue-baste in place, matching edge of header with raw edge of fabric. Begin and end on straight grain of fabric. Since round table covers are partially cut on the bias, take care not to stretch braid or fabric when stitching. Stitch braid in place with a zipper foot $3/8$" (1 cm) from edge. Leave 3" (7.5 cm) free at each end.

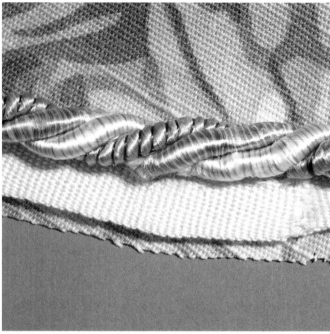

To finish braid ends, untwist braid, clipping strands apart to separate. Tape strand ends to prevent raveling. Trim braid tape ends to 1" (2.5 cm) and overlap. Pin or glue-baste in place.

Retwist braid ends together to form one continuous piece. With a fabric glue stick or hand-tacking, secure twisted ends in place and continue stitching braid to table skirt.

### TIPS

• There are any number of other ways to finish table toppers and skirts: Add a ruffled border to the hem of the skirt for a romantic feminine accent. Another suggestion is to cut and hem a bias strip 4" (10 cm) wide from same fabric as topper. Position top edge of strip 6" (15 cm) above skirt hem and pin in place. Fold under joining ends and stitch. Stitch along top edge of band, attaching it to skirt.

• Following instructions for a circular table skirt (page 101), make a circular topper with a 3"-6" (7.5 cm-15 cm) drop on all edges.

• Consider using large bedsheets for seamless large table skirts or tablecloths.

• Look for easy-care, as well as wrinkle-, and stain-resistant fabrics.

To stitch front and back of skirt together, pin skirts with right sides together and raw edges even, placing pins 3"- 4" (7.5 cm -10 cm) apart. Place front and back panel seams at right angles or adjacent to one another to eliminate the extra bulk of double seam allowances. Stitch together with a zipper foot.

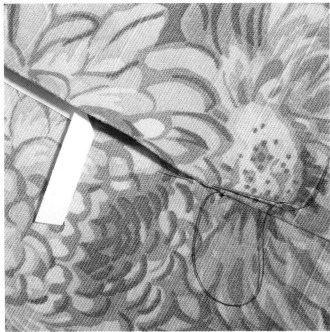

Flip fabric to side with first stitching holding the braid in place and stitch again. This time crowd the braid, stitching as close to the braid as possible. This will produce a neat, professional finish. Trim seam allowance to 1/4" (6 mm). Turn skirt right side out through opening.

To finish, fuse opening closed with fusible tape to help match the design, and slipstitch.

## SIMPLE HEMS

To make a *mock-welted hem,* construct reversible skirt, omitting braid. Do not close opening. Cut cable cord to circumference of skirt. Glue or stitch ends together. Insert cable cord through opening and hand-baste cording in place through both thicknesses. Stitch close to cording, using a zipper foot. Slipstitch or fuse opening closed.

To *serge-finish hem,* cut and seam panels for front and back, omitting the opening. Pin skirts with *wrong* sides together and raw edges even. Using decorative thread in the loopers, serge edges together with a short stitch length, trimming 1/2" (1.3 cm) at edges.

In place of decorative braid, finish hem with a mock-welted edge, or serge-finish.

# CHAPTER 6

# Bedrooms and Bedclothes

As evening approaches, retreating to your own private space is a welcome respite from the demands of the day. A sense of peace and harmony should prevail in a room where comfort comes first. Pamper yourself in beautiful surroundings with sumptuous fabrics and the special bedroom fashions that create an ambiance of luxury. Making your own bed coverings, including dust ruffles, shams, and pillows, allows you to create your own fantasy. If you have a passion for frills, enhance the room with inviting ruffles and flourishes. Or, if you favor a more tailored look, use pleats and welting.

# Duvet or Comforter Cover

A bed sets the style and mood in the bedroom. Give your bed a cozy, custom touch with a duvet or comforter cover. Make your cover with one fabric and build the rest of your room around it, or make it reversible with a different fabric on each side for two coordinating looks. Adding braid or piping will give a professional finish.

# Reversible Duvet Cover

## CLOSURES

## MATERIALS

- Decorator fabric for duvet front
- Contrasting decorator fabric for duvet back
- Twisted braid with heading tape
- Desired closure, either two zippers each 22" (56 cm) long, snap tape, hook-and-loop tape, or ³/₄" (20 mm) buttons

## CUTTING

Measure your duvet or comforter. Note any deviations from standard measurements. Allow extra fabric for matching prints. If fabric is not wide enough, cut two panels in desired length. If necessary, piece a panel by cutting one panel in half lengthwise and stitching it to either side of center panel. Cut out to required measurements.

Cut front and back 1" (2.5 cm) larger than the length and width of the duvet or comforter plus closure allowance. For zipper closure, add 2" (5 cm) to the back length; for button closure, add 7¹/₂" (19 cm) to back length. Trim corner curves if desired.

For snap or hook-and-loop tape closures, cut tapes 44" (112 cm) long and an 11" x 44" (28 cm x 112 cm) front facing for all sizes.

## STANDARD DUVET AND COMFORTER MEASUREMENTS

TWIN: 66" x 86" (168 cm x 218 cm); 64" x 90" (163 cm x 229 cm)
FULL/QUEEN: 86" x 86" (218 cm x 218 cm); 84" x 90" (213 cm x 229 cm)
KING: 102" x 86" (259 cm x 218 cm); 101" x 94" (256 cm x 239 cm)

Zipper, snap tape, and hook-and-loop tape all are excellent closures for a duvet or comforter cover. They usually are applied at the bottom back.

**Back zipper closure:** From lower edge, press up 3" (7.5 cm) to right side. Baste 1" (2.5 cm) from fold. Cut along the pressed edge. Mark centered 44" (112 cm) for zippers. Stitch from markings to ends. Following manufacturer's instructions for a lapped closure, insert zippers with zipper pulls meeting at center.

**Snap tape closure:** With a zipper foot, stitch ball section of snap tape with ball centered to right side of bottom (foot) cover back seam allowance on the seamline. Serge or zigzag seam allowance close to stitching, taking care not to cut tape. Turn tape to wrong side and stitch in place close to remaining edge. To make front facing flap, with right sides together, press in half lengthwise and stitch short ends together with a ¹/₂" (1.3 cm)

seam. Turn right side out and press. With one socket centered, stitch tape to facing ⁵/₈" (1.5 cm) from front raw edge. Center facing, tape side up and pin to front cover seam allowance with raw edges even. Stitch ¹/₂" (1.3 cm) from edge.

**Hook-and-loop closure:** Stitch hook-and-loop tape in place same as for snap tape.

**Button closure:** Mark 15" (38 cm) up from bottom edge of cover back and cut across width. Allow 42" (107 cm) centered for opening. Press 1¹/₂" (3.8 cm) to wrong side twice along both raw edges. Stitch hems in place close to folded edge. Stitch ⁷/₈" (2.2 cm) long buttonholes parallel to fold at 10" (25.5 cm) to 12" (30.5 cm) intervals. Sew buttons to match on other side.

Button closures add a European design element to a duvet or comforter cover. Choose flat buttons and place the opening near the lower edge of the cover.

## ADDING TWISTED BRAID

Matching raw edges, stitch braid to duvet front with a 3/8" (1 cm) seam allowance. Clip braid heading to ease around curved corners.

### ASSEMBLY

Stitch comforter or duvet cover front and back together with a 1/2" (1.3 cm) seam allowance, adding braid if desired, and backstitching at closure bottom seam opening edges. Apply desired closure. Turn right side out, press, and insert duvet or comforter. Fasten closure.

### TABS

To stop duvet from shifting inside the cover, use corner snaps to secure. If duvet does not have snaps, add them at corners. An alternative is to secure duvet to cover seam allowance with hand-worked French hanging tacks, 1" (2.5 cm) long, at each corner.

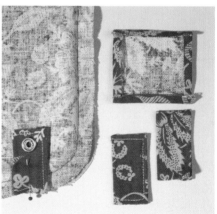

Cut four tabs 2 1/2" (6.5 cm) square. Press 1/4" (6 mm) under on all sides. Fold in half, wrong sides together, with pressed edges even; edgestitch. Attach snap. Align tabs with duvet snaps, pin tabs to inside of cover. Stitch in place.

# Bed Skirts

While originally designed to cover and protect the box spring, dust ruffles or bed skirts are another way to add a colorful dimension to your bedroom decorating scheme. Double the ruffles for a country look; pleat the skirt for a tailored look.

# Skirt Bases

Bed skirts are easy to custom fit for any bed. Make one continuous skirt or, for beds with a footboard, make the skirt in three separate sections. Each unit is constructed by attaching the skirt to a base of either a fitted sheet or a deck, which is a flat sheet or piece of fabric cut to the size of the box spring top plus hems. The bases are interchangeable. The sheet or fabric must be sturdy enough to bear the weight of the skirt. Bed skirts are attached only to the sides and foot of the bed. The head is left unskirted.

## STANDARD BOX SPRING SIZES

| | |
|---|---|
| TWIN | 38" x 74" (96.5 cm x 188 cm) |
| FULL | 54" x 74" (137 cm x 188 cm) |
| QUEEN | 60" x 80" (152 cm x 203 cm) |
| KING | 76" x 80" (193 cm x203 cm) |

Add 1" (2.5 cm) to width and 4 1/2" (11.5 cm) to length of box spring measurement for seam allowances and hems.

## FITTED SHEET

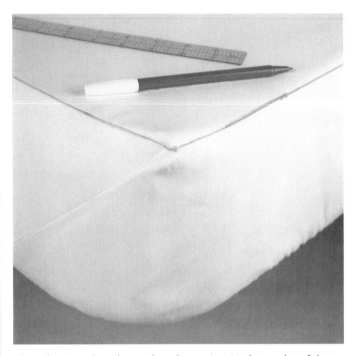

Place sheet evenly and securely on box spring. Mark top edge of sheet along side and bottom edges, using a fabric marker and ruler. Remove sheet and mark a parallel line 1/2" (1.3 cm) down toward floor from previous marking. Mark center of each side and bottom edge.

## CUSTOMIZED DECK

If needed, cut and stitch deck panels together to fit top of box spring with a 2" (5 cm) double hem at upper edge. To round corners, make a cardboard template, using a 7" (18 cm) diameter plate as a guide.

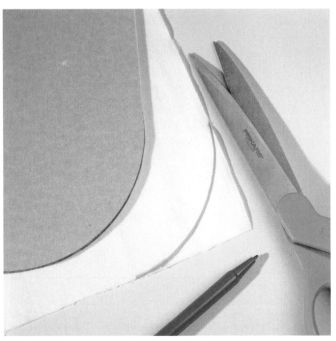

Fold deck in half lengthwise, with corners even. With disappearing marker, mark corners at lower edge using template and cut out along marked line.

# Gathered Dust Ruffles

For gathered dust ruffles, you can cut your fabric on the lengthwise or crosswise grain. It will depend on your fabric design and the number of seams you wish to make.

## CUTTING

To determine yardage, add width of box spring plus twice the length. Allow 2 to 3 times this length for gathers, depending on the fabric weight. For lightweight fabrics allow more; for heavier fabrics, allow less. Measure drop from top of boxspring to floor, and add $4^1/2"$ (11.5 cm) for hems and seams.

**For crosswise cutting,** take the total dust ruffle length and divide it by the fabric width to determine the number of drop sections needed. Round up any fractions.

Multiply this number by the length of the drops to determine the total fabric amount needed. Divide by 36" (100 cm) for yards (meters).

**For lengthwise cutting,** determine how many full drops fit into your fabric width. Divide this number into the total dust ruffle length needed, including seam and hem allowances. This will give the total fabric amount needed. Divide by 36" (100 cm) for yards (meters).

## STANDARD DUST RUFFLE

Measure and cut dust ruffle, adding 3" (7.5 cm) for double hems at each end. Stitch all dust ruffle skirt sections together and press seams open. Make a 2" (5 cm) double hem along lower edge and a $1^1/2"$ (3.8 cm) double hem at each end.

Stitch gathering stitches along top edge (see Chapter One, Ruffling Techniques). Mark centers of foot edge and sides of ruffle and deck. Beginning at one upper cor-

ner, pin ruffle to deck, matching center markings. Pull up gathers to fit.

Zigzag in place with $3/8"$ (1 cm) seam allowances and stitch again with a straight stitch $1/2"$ (13 mm) from cut edges. Trim and press seams toward deck. Topstitch seam allowances to deck.

## SPLIT-CORNER DUST RUFFLE

Measure and cut three sections, two sides and one foot, allowing for $1^1/2"$ (3.8 cm) double hems at each end. Stitch skirt sections together if necessary. Press seams open. Hem ruffle with 2" (5 cm) double hems at lower edge and $1^1/2"$ (3.8 cm) end hems. Mark centers of each ruffle section and each side and foot edge of deck. With right sides together, and with ends extending $1^1/2"$ (3.8 cm) beyond each foot corner, pin skirt sections to deck, matching center markings. Pull up gathers to fit. Stitch in place as for Standard Dust Ruffle.

Trim to $1/4"$ (6 mm) and press seams toward deck. To reinforce seam, topstitch seam allowances to deck.

For split-corner dust ruffle, pin bottom skirt section to deck, overlapping top edge end hems $1^1/2"$ (3.8 cm). Zigzag-stitch using $3/8"$ (1 cm) seam allowances. Straight-stitch using $1/2"$ (1.3 cm) seam allowances.

# Doubled Gathered Dust Ruffle

See photo, page 109. Make double dust ruffle using two different fabrics with top layer 4" (10 cm) shorter than bottom. Cut either continuous or split-corner dust ruffles, allowing for 1½" (3.5 cm) double hems at ends and 4½" (11.5 cm) for hems and seam allowances. Stitch sections together if necessary. Hem lower edge with 2" (5 cm) double hems and ends with 1½" (3.8 cm) double hems.

Place top ruffle over bottom ruffle with cut edges and end hems even. Gather as one. Stitch to fitted sheet or deck.

# Detachable Gathered Dust Ruffle

This technique allows you to easily remove a dust ruffle from the mattress without having to disassemble the bed. Hook-and-loop tape is applied to the fitted sheet or deck and to the band on the dust ruffle. This method also prevents the dust ruffle from shifting position while on the bed.

## MATERIALS

■ Decorator fabric
■ Fitted sheet or cotton sheeting for deck
■ Fabric for band
■ Hook-and-loop tape

## ASSEMBLY

Cut dust ruffle and stitch sections together following directions for Standard Dust Ruffle. Divide into quarters and mark. Cut bands 4" (10 cm) wide and the length of three sides of the box spring plus 2" (5 cm). Stitch band sections together. To finish band, make a 1" (2.5 cm) single hem along each short end. With wrong sides together, press band in half lengthwise and mark quarter sections.

Gather dust ruffle and with right sides together, pin to one long edge of band, matching markings and raw edges. Zigzag ruffle to band with a ³/₈" (1 cm) seam allowance. Straight-stitch again with a ½" (1.3 cm) seam allowance. Press seam toward band. Fold ½" (1.3 cm) under on remaining long edge of band and edgestitch over seamline, covering ruffle seam allowance inside band.

Attach loop side of tape to wrong side of band, placing one edge along seamline. Attach hook side inside marking on fitted sheet so that it lies flat on top of box spring. Cut tape at corners and miter for a smooth finish. Attach dust ruffle to fitted sheet with hook and loop fasteners.

# Pleated Bed Skirt

Cut bed skirt allowing 12" (30.5 cm) for each pleat and 1$\frac{1}{2}$" (3.8 cm) double hems at ends. Allow for four pleats, one on each side and one at each of the bed foot corners. Allow more pleats for a large bed if desired. Stitch skirt sections together, pressing seams open. Stitch a 2" (5 cm) double hem at the floor edge and 1$\frac{1}{2}$" (3.8 cm) double side hems.

## TIPS

• Make a series of box pleats 4" (10 cm) along all sides.
• Sew pleats every 8" (20.5 cm) along all sides. Attach a tassel at the seamline between each pleat.
• Line each pleat with contrasting fabric, either solid or a print. Allow for seam allowances on both front edges of each pleat.
• Outline each pleat with ribbon by attaching to outside edges. Miter upper corner to form a point over the pleat. Add an additional line of ribbon across bottom hem edge connecting each pleat.
• At bottom corners, tack each pleat back and affix with a button so that pleats are held open.
• Before stitching pleat, add ruffled lace to the inside back edge.
• Decorate each pleat with a ribbon bow, matching or contrasting fabric bow, tassels, or buttons.
• Restrict pleats to corners at foot of bed to accommodate large-size fabric prints and motifs.

On right side, make pleats in skirt, centering pleats on each side and bottom corners at markings. Mark beginning and end of each 12" (30.5 cm) pleat. Make another mark 3" (7.5 cm) in from each side of pleat marks. Press across skirt at markings as shown. Baste across upper edge. To prevent pleats from shifting at lower edge, hold in place with masking tape.

Mark $\frac{1}{2}$" (1.3 cm) down from marking on fitted sheet. Mark pleat position on sheet. With right sides together, pin skirt in place, matching raw edges to second marking. At corners, pin pleat in place, clipping at corner to basting stitches. Stitch in place $\frac{1}{2}$" (1.3 cm) from raw edge.

# Pillowcases and Shams

A covey of pillows to sink into, especially when covered in beautifully decorated pillowcases and shams, makes any bed more inviting. Make them plain, ruffled, flanged, or double-flanged, and add elegant accents such as lace, eyelet, and embroidery.

While there are standard pillow sizes for sleeping, there is no restriction on the sizes of pillows that can be used to dress a bed. You can make decorated sleeping pillows in standard sizes (see box below) by using the techniques in this section, as well as pillows in the sizes of your choice.

| STANDARD PILLOW SIZES | |
|---|---|
| STANDARD: | 20" x 26" (51 cm x 66 cm) |
| QUEEN: | 20" x 30" (51 cm x 76 cm) |
| KING: | 20" x 36" (51 cm x 91.5 cm) |

Clockwise from top right:
Eyelet ruffle-edged pillowcase, pillowcase with eyelet envelope flap, pillow sham with classic flange, embroidered eyelet pillowcase, and pillow sham with double flange.

## Eyelet Ruffle–Edged Pillowcase

### MATERIALS

■ Pillowcase fabric
■ Pregathered eyelet trim

### ASSEMBLY

Cut fabric double the width of the pillow plus 1" (2.5 cm) by the length plus 2" (5 cm). Cut pregathered eyelet the same width measurement.

To attach ruffle, refold hem twice over header stitching, press and pin in place. Stitch along the pressed edge. Turn hem to inside and press. Topstitch over hem allowance with a straight or decorative stitch. With right sides together, serge or zigzag-stitch along the remaining edges. Turn right side out and insert pillow.

Press ½" (1.3 cm) to right side twice along one long edge. Open out pressed edge and place gathered edge of eyelet trim along inside second pressed line. Stitch eyelet trim in place.

# Envelope Pillowcase with Embroidered Eyelet Flap

### MATERIALS

- Lightweight fabric, such as batiste or lawn
- Fabric with embroidered edge

### ASSEMBLY

Measure pillow length and add $1/2$" (1.3 cm). Measure width and add 1" (2.5 cm). Cut a pillowcase front and back. For envelope flap, try this suggestion: First make a plan on freezer paper. Draw four triangles with embroidered bases to create flap shown in photo on page 115. Then cut them out from eyelet, allowing $1/2$" (1.3 cm) seam allowances.

Press $1/2$" (1.3 cm) to wrong side twice along one long edge of front. Stitch in place along folded edge. With right sides together and raw edges matching, pin flap to top edge of back. Serge or zigzag raw edges. With right sides together and matching raw edges, serge or zigzag along three sides with $1/4$" (6 mm)

seams, leaving top edge open. Turn right side out and insert pillow. Place flap over pillowcase front.

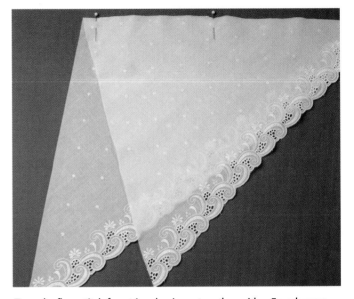

To make flap, stitch four triangle pieces together with a French seam. Press seams toward center.

# Classic Flanged Pillow Sham

### MATERIALS

- Decorator fabric
- Batting
- Lining fabric, such as muslin, cotton, or cotton blend

### ASSEMBLY

To make a 4" (10 cm) flange, measure pillow and add 9" (23 cm) to front. For back with a lapped opening, cut one overlap section the pillow width with flange plus 1" (2.5 cm) and half the pillow length with flange plus $5^1/2$" (14 cm). Cut an underlap section the pillow width with flange plus 1" (2.5 cm) and half the length with flange plus $1^1/2$" (3.8 cm). Cut batting and lining same as front.

Place batting on wrong side of front, place lining right side up, over batting. Pin and baste $3/8$" (1 cm) inside cut edges. Trim batting. For back overlap section, press under 5" (12.5 cm) to wrong side along overlap edge and blind-hem. On underlap, make a 1" (2.5 cm) hem on one long edge and machine blind-hem in place. With right sides together, place back overlap over front, matching three sides. Pin back

underlap *over* remaining side of front with hemmed edges overlapping and sides matching. Serge or zigzag-stitch $1/2$" (1.3 cm) seam allowances around edges. Clip corners and turn right side out and press.

Mark 4" (10 cm) inside finished edges with a disappearing fabric marker. Top-stitch along marking through all layers. Insert pillow.

# Embroidered Eyelet Pillowcase

Beautiful eyelet embroidered fabric with decorative edgings is perfect for use in a bedroom. This simple pillowcase highlights the embroidered edging.

## MATERIALS

- Eyelet fabric with embroidered edge

## ASSEMBLY

With embroidered edge along one end, cut pillowcase to pillow length plus 2 1/2" (6.5 cm) by twice the pillow width plus 1" (2.5 cm). Fold fabric in half crosswise with right sides together. Serge or zigzag along two sides with 1/2" (1.3 cm) seam. Turn right side out and press.

# Double-Flanged Pillow Sham

## MATERIALS

- Decorator fabric
- Batting same size as pillow width and length
- Lining fabric
- Zipper

Cut pillow front 10" (25.5 cm) larger than pillow all around. Cut back length 12" (30.5 cm) larger than pillow length for zipper closure and 4" (10 cm) double flange. Pillow back width is 10" (25.5 cm) larger than pillow. Cut batting and lining for front.

Place batting on wrong side of front and place lining right side up over batting to sandwich batting between lining and front. Pin and baste 3/8" (1 cm) from edges. Trim batting close to stitching. Cut back in half crosswise and baste edges together with a 1" (2.5 cm) seam allowance. Insert zipper following manufacturer's instructions. *Open zipper partway.*

To form flange, press 5" (12.5 cm) to wrong side along outer edges of front and back. Open out corners. Press corners to wrong side diagonally so first pressed lines match.

Open out fold and with right sides together, refold diagonally through center of corner so raw edges match. Mark a line along second pressed fold (on right angle to corner) and stitch. Trim seam allowance to 3/8" (1 cm) and press seam open. Repeat for all front and back corners.

Turn corners right side out and press. With wrong sides together, pin front to back, matching mitered corners. Mark 4" (10 cm) inside finished edges with a disappearing fabric marker. Topstitch along marking through all layers. Insert pillow through zipper.

## TIPS

- For a fuller look to the double flange, add batting to both back and front.
- Use a contrast fabric to line both inside flange edges facing one another.
- Add a gathered lace or eyelet ruffle between flanges on all edges before stitching.
- Decorate flange stitching line with ribbon, embroidery, or other decorative trim.
- Attach large self-covered buttons to the corners of the flanges at the stitching line.

# Optional Lace Overlay

## MATERIALS

- Decorator fabric
- Lace yardage
- Zipper
- Masking tape

Add a lace overlay to a solid-color pillow cover for an attractive pillow with a distinctly feminine feel.

## ASSEMBLY

Cut decorator fabric front and lace — with careful attention to lace motif placement — 1" (2. 5 cm) larger than pillow front on all sides. Cut back 2" (5 cm) longer than front for zipper closure and 1" (2. 5 cm) wider. Insert zipper in center back. *Open zipper partway.*

Place right side of lace over right side of front. Pin in place and use masking tape to prevent lace from shifting.

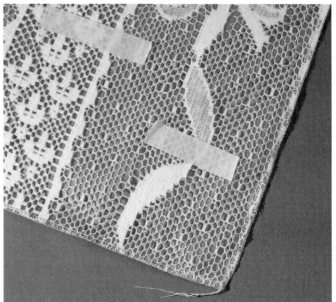

Machine-baste or serge layers together. With right sides together, serge or zigzag front to back with 1/2" (1.3 cm) seams. Trim seams and clip corners. Turn right side out and insert pillow.

# Shirr Magic

Create a striking room dressing with fabric that drapes over your walls to creatively hide flaws, provide warmth, and add insulation. This designer look is easy to achieve with sew-on shirred or smocking tapes that have built-in hook-and-loop fasteners. This method allows you to remove the coverings for cleaning.

# Shirred Walls

## MATERIALS

- Decorator fabric
- Self-adhesive hook and loop shirring tape system
- Plastic cord locks

## CUTTING

Measure wall surface to be covered. Allow two and a half times the finished width of the wall for fullness, 1/2" (1.3 cm) for seams, 2" (5 cm) for each side hem, and 8" (20 cm) for top and bottom hems. Divide this measurement by the fabric width for the number of panels. Multiply the number of panels by the wall length and divide by 36" (91.5 cm) to get the amount of yardage. Purchase additional fabric for matching prints and repeats.

Cut fabric into required number of lengths. Cut shirring/loop tape the width of the gathered fabric plus 3" (7.5 cm). Cut hook tape the width of the wall.

## ASSEMBLY

With right sides together, stitch fabric lengths together at sides with 1/2" (1.3 cm) seam allowances. Press seams open. Hem bottom with a 2" (5 cm) double hem. Make 1" (2.5 cm) double side hems. With wrong sides together, fold down top hem 4" (10 cm) and press. Pin wrong side of tape over raw edge of top hem, 1/2" (1.3 cm) from folded edge, with loop side of the tape facing up. Stitch tape in place along top and bottom edges, being careful not to catch cords. Knot ends of cords securely in an overhand knot at one side. Apply to hook tape.

# Vanities and Sink Skirts

Self adhesive hook-and-loop tape makes it easy to dress up any ordinary table as a vanity. One pretty application is to cover the top in the same fabric and lay a glass top over it. Affix hook tape to side of table. Start the top of your shirred skirt at glass edge. The best placement for a sink is to place the skirt low enough that it won't get wet, or affix it to the underside of the sink.

Measure the distance between the top of the vanity

To gather shirring tape, hold cords on one side and gently push fabric toward the opposite end. Push fabric as far as it will go and distribute fullness evenly. Secure excess cords with stopper.

Adhere hook fastener tape to wall and mount fabric, adjusting shirring and redistributing fullness.

or the desired position on the sink and the floor. Add 2¹/₂" (6.5 cm) for hems. Follow manufacturer's instructions for fabric width. Hem sides with ¹/₂" (1.3 cm) double hem, then press 1" (2.5 cm) to wrong side twice on lower edge and stitch in place for lower hem. Press ¹/₂" (1.3 cm) to wrong side along top edge. Place wrong side of shirring loop tape over raw edge of top hem, ¹/₄" (6 mm) from top edge. Stitch tape in place along top and bottom edges, being careful not to catch cords. Gather to fit vanity or sink and secure cord ends. Adhere hook tape to surface and mount fabric.

To add richness to a vanity skirt, make the length slightly longer so that it puddles gently on the floor. Select a crisp fabric.

Recess skirt below the edge of a sink to prevent contact with water. The area behind the skirt provides subtle storage.

## TIPS

- Knot ends of shirring cords to prevent them from being pulled out.
- *We suggest not cutting excess cords* so that fabric may be released from the gathers for easy care and cleaning.
- For an alternate sink application, attach the skirt to the underside of the sink lip. Adhere the hook tape to the underside of the sink lip. Attach loop tape to the front of the skirt instead of the back.

# Glossary

## A

**Appliqué** — A fabric motif added to the right side of a base fabric by stitching, bonding or both.

**Apron** — The wood trim below the window sill.

**Arched Window** — A semicircular window usually over another window or door. Often called a Palladian window.

## B

**Bar Tack** — Reinforcement stitching worked over and over in the same place by hand or machine to secure facings or closures.

**Batting** — Layer of polyester or natural "fleece" used to wrap, back, and pad a surface.

**Bias** — A diagonal line between the lengthwise and crosswise grain of fabric. True bias is 45 degrees to the selvage and is the direction of the greatest stretch.

**Blindstitch** — Used to anchor hems. Machine-stitch option used with a blindhem foot to make several straight stitches followed by one zigzag stitch, catching the hem.

**Brush Fringe** — Also called moss fringe. Short, thick luxurious fringe on a heading that is normally enclosed in a seam.

## C

**Cable Cord** — The white cord $1/8"$ to $1"$ (3 mm to 2.5 cm) in diameter, usually enclosed in fabric to create piping or welting.

**Casing** — For curtains, also called a rod pocket. A fabric tunnel formed by folding the top of the curtain under and stitching.

**Comforter** — Natural- or synthetic-filled bed covering that can be tufted or quilted.

## D

**Deck** — The flat hidden surface under seat cushions or above box springs to which decorative skirts are attached.

**Drapery Weights** — Square, round or chain weights specifically designed to help maintain the hanging shape of pleats and folds.

**Duvet** — A down-, feather-, or polyester-filled channelled bed covering that is thicker than a comforter. Usually protected by a removable cover.

## E

**Edgestitch** – Machine stitching close to a finished edge or seamline, usually a scant $1/8"$ (3 mm) from the edge.

## F

**Fabric Glue** — Specially formulated glue for bonding fabrics.

**Favoring** — A method of rolling a seam to the lining side so the lining does not show on the outside. Often used for lined window treatments. Serging seams facilitates favoring.

**Fiberfill** — Stuffing material used for filling pillows and pillow forms.

**Fleece** — A dense form of batting used to add loft and resilience to various surfaces. Also available as a fusible.

**Fusible Web** — Heat-sensitive non-woven adhesive fibers placed between two layers of fabric for bonding. Available as a sheet or tape, and/or with a paper backing. See also Paper-backed Fusible Web.

## G

**Grain** — The lengthwise and crosswise threads of a woven fabric. Lengthwise grain is parallel to the selvage and more stable than the crosswise grain which is perpendicular to the selvage.

## H

**Heading** — The ruffled portion at the top of a shirred curtain. Also refers to the top portion of a curtain with self-styling tape and the top portion of an applied ruffle.

**Hemstitching** — A traditional hand method for hemming, now worked by machine with a wing needle and decorative stitch designs.

**Holdbacks** — Hardware mounted on the window frame or wall for holding a window treatment, including a window scarf.

**Hook-and-Loop Tape** — A pull-apart fastener with one side consisting of numerous small hooks, and the other with loops, available as a sew-on or self-adhesive. Some self-styling curtain tapes come with hook-and-loop backings.

## J

**Jabots** — The cascading side pieces that accompany a draped swag window treatment.

## L

**Lambrequin** — A decorative wooden frame that extends down both sides of the window, usually padded and covered with fabric.

## M

**Meeting Rails** — The two horizontal pieces where double-hung window sashes meet and overlap at the center.

**Mitering Corners** — Finishing corners with a seam at a 45 degree angle for decorative effect or to reduce bulk.

**Moss Fringe** — See Brush Fringe.

**Mock Welting** — Simulated welting made by sewing cable cord inside an edge.

**Mounting Board** — A fabric-covered board for securing window treatments.

**Mullions** — The wooden horizontal and vertical cross pieces dividing a window.

### N

**Narrow Hem** — A hem created by turning 1/4" (6 mm) under twice and stitching. Can be stitched by hand or with machine attachments.

### O

**Overlock machine** — See Serger.

### P

**Palladian Window** — See Arched Window.

**Paper-backed Fusible Web** — Heat-sensitive non-woven adhesive fibers applied to a peel-away release paper backing, used for bonding fabric. Available as a sheet or a tape.

**Pelmet** — A shaped flat valance.

**Piping** — Decorative edging composed of narrow fabric-covered cable cord.

**Puddling** — Allowing fabric to pool on the floor by making hems longer than floor length.

### R

**Railroading** — Changing a cutting layout so that fabric pieces run along the lengthwise grain rather than crosswise, to eliminate the need for piecing.

**Repeats** — The vertical distance between identical fabric motifs.

**Return** — The continuation of a window treatment, and the distance, from the front edge to the wall.

**Rod Pocket** — See Casing.

**Roman Shade** — A shade that creates horizontal folds when drawn up with a system of threaded rings and cords. It hangs flat when not drawn.

### S

**Sashes** — The upper or lower moving sections of a window, sometimes divided with mullions.

**Self-styling Tapes** — Sew-on tapes with cords that when drawn up will produce various types of designs, such as shirring, pleating, and smocking.

**Serger** — A machine that stitches, trims and finishes in one step, and uses from two to five threads, making up to 1500 stitches per minute. Also called an overlock machine.

**Scarf** — A length of fabric draped over holdbacks or a curtain rod.

**Sill** — The horizontal bottom portion of the window frame above the apron.

**Slipstitch** — A hand stitch formed by guiding the needle through a folded edge, then picking up a thread of the fabric underneath.

**Stack Back Mounting** — See Stacking Space. Mounting of draperies on either side of a window, allowing maximum glass exposure when curtains are fully opened.

**Stacking Space** — The amount of space beside the window taken up by draperies when curtains are fully opened.

**Stitch-in-the Ditch** — Stitching directly into the groove of a previously stitched seamline on the right side through all layers.

**Straight of Grain** — The direction parallel to the lengthwise or crosswise grain. In purchased patterns it usually refers to lengthwise grain.

**Swag** — A draped length of fabric secured to a rod or mounting board, sometimes accompanied by jabots.

### T

**Tiebacks** — Used to hold curtains or draperies back to the side of the window. Can be fabric, twisted braid, or hardware.

**Topstitch** — Stitching on the right side of fabric to secure an edge and act as a decorative accent, usually 1/4" (6 mm) or more away from the edge.

**Trim** — Various fringes, braids, piping and welting used as embellishment.

**Twisted Braid** — A braid with or without a header and made of twisted cords.

### V

**Valance** — A short, decorative window treatment placed over draperies or curtains, or used alone.

### W

**Welting** — Fabric-covered cable cord larger than 1/4" (6 mm) in diameter. Used for a decorative edging, and sometimes called cording.

**Wing Needle** — A sewing machine needle with flanged sides that separate fabric threads, creating openwork while hemstitching.

# Index

# Acknowledgments

**Project Designers and Samplemakers**
Joan Greenhut, Virginia Jansen, Nancy Keller, Karen Kunkel

**Special thanks to**
Elaine Gross, Kathryn Nelson, Linda Weiss

**Contributors**
Sewing machines and sergers courtesy of Bernina of America

**Photography**
*Photographers* Andy Cohen, Lawrence E. Cohen, Geoffrey Gross, Frank Kuo
*Photo Stylists* Michael Cannarozzi, Patricia O'Shaughnessy

Photographed at Studio One Productions and on location

Additional photography courtesy of: Butterick, pages 38, 41, 78, 81; DuPont, page 11; Vogue, pages 68, 72-73, 75, 80, 82, 83, 99, 104-105; Waverly, division of F. Shumacher & Co., pages 22-23, 28, 54, 88-89, 109, 114, 121 (top and bottom)

Notions and equipment courtesy of Coats & Clark; Dritz; E-Z International; Fairfield Processing Corp.; Fiskars; Voster Marketing Spaceboards

Hardware courtesy of Graber Industries; Kirsch; Marmelstein

Trims courtesy of Conso Products Co.; C. M. Offray & Sons, Inc.; William E. Wright Co.

Fabrics courtesy of Ametex Inc.; Bloomcraft, Inc.; Braemore; Concord; Cyrus Clark Co. Inc.; Covington Fabrics Corp.; P. Kaufmann, Inc.; Richloom; Spectrum; Springs Industries; James Thompson & Co., Inc.; Waverly, division of F. Shumacher & Co.

# Pattern Listing

The following is a list of the patterns featured in this book.

Page 38 Draped scarf, Butterick 5480

Page 41 Swag and jabots, Butterick 5480

Page 51 Shaped valance, Vogue 1081

Page 68 Pillows, Vogue 7955

Pages 72-73, 75 Cover-ups, Vogue 2837

Page 78 Folding chair cover, Butterick 3104

Page 80 Chair cover with button accents, Vogue 1216

Page 81 Ruffled chair cover, Butterick 3104

Page 82 Straight-back chair cover, Vogue 2374

Page 83 Chaise lounge cover, Vogue 1156

Page 99 Reversible table ensemble, Vogue 2908

Page 104-105 Bedroom ensemble, Vogue 2908

Due to changes beyond our control, over time, these patterns may no longer be available. When this happens, call 1-800-766-3619 to order the pattern. Limited stock is kept for one year from the date the pattern is discontinued. For further information, call Consumer Services, 1-800-766-2670. To order your free pattern, fill in the coupon on page 127.